PENGUIN BOOKS

The Commission for Africa

In 2004, the Commission for Africa was formed by 17 people, brought together to define the challenges facing Africa, and to provide clear recommendations on the changes that are needed to reduce poverty. The majority are from Africa, and have varied experience as political leaders, public servants, and in the private sector. The Commission is: Tony Blair (Chair), Fola Adeola, K Y Amoako, Nancy Kassebaum Baker, Hilary Benn, Gordon Brown, Michel Camdessus, Bob Geldof, Ralph Goodale, Ji Peiding, William Kalema, Trevor Manuel, Benjamin Mkapa, Linah Mohohlo, Tidjane Thiam, Anna Tibaijuka and Meles Zenawi.

Our Common Interest

The Commission for Africa

An Argument

PENGUIN BOOKS

PENGUIN BOOKS

Published by the Penguin Group
Penguin Books Ltd, 80 Strand, London WC2R 0RL, England
Penguin Group (USA) Inc., 375 Hudson Street, New York, New York 10014, USA
Penguin Group (Canada), 90 Eglinton Avenue East, Suite 700, Toronto,
Ontario, Canada M4P 3YZ (a division of Pearson Penguin Canada Inc.)
Penguin Ireland, 25 St Stephen's Green, Dublin 2, Ireland (a division of Penguin Books Ltd)
Penguin Group (Australia), 250 Camberwell Road, Camberwell, Victoria 3124, Australia
(a division of Pearson Australia Group Pty Ltd)
Penguin Books India Pvt Ltd, 11 Community Centre, Panchsheel Park,
New Delhi – 110 017, India
Penguin Group (NZ), cnr Airborne and Rosedale Roads, Albany,
Auckland 1310, New Zealand (a division of Pearson New Zealand Ltd)
Penguin Books (South Africa) (Pty) Ltd, 24 Sturdee Avenue,
Rosebank 2196, South Africa

Penguin Books Ltd, Registered Offices: 80 Strand, London WC2R 0RL, England

www.penguin.com

First published by the Commission for Africa March 2005
Published in Penguin Books 2005

7

Copyright © Commission for Africa, 2005
All rights reserved

The moral right of the authors has been asserted

Set in 11/13 pt Monotype Bembo
Typeset by Rowland Phototypesetting Ltd, Bury St Edmunds, Suffolk

Printed in England by Clays Ltd, St Ives plc

Contents

Introduction

About this report

This year is of great significance for Africa. In 2005 the world will review progress on a remarkable commitment it made in 2000. The Millennium Development Goals set out to halve world poverty by 2015. But we are now a third of the way to that date and the rich world is falling behind on its pledges to the poor. Nowhere is that more clear than in Africa, where the world is furthest behind in progress to fulfil those solemn promises. If that is to change we must act now.

But all is not gloom. For 2005 is also the year in which it is becoming clear to the outside world that things are changing on the continent – with African governments showing a new vision, both individually and working together through the African Union and its New Partnership for Africa's Development (NEPAD) programme. Africa, at last, looks set to deliver.

A year ago, the British Prime Minister, Tony Blair, brought together 17 people to form a Commission for Africa. We were invited in our individual and personal capacities rather than as representatives of governments or institutions. A majority of us come from Africa and we have varied experience as political leaders, public servants and in the private sector.

The task we were set was this: to define the challenges facing Africa, and to provide clear recommendations on how to support the changes needed to reduce poverty.

Our starting point was the recognition that Africa must drive its own development. Rich nations should support that, because it is in our common interest to make the world a more prosperous and secure place – though the international community will contribute to the achievement of these objectives in different ways. But what is clear is that if Africa does not create the right conditions for development, then any amount of outside support will fail.

Our recommendations are based on two things. We carefully studied all the evidence available to find out what is working and what is not. And we consulted extensively, inside and outside Africa, with governments, civil society, the academic world and with those in the public and private sector.

We have met individuals and groups from each region and 49 individual countries in Africa, and from every G8 country, China, India and across Europe. We have received nearly 500 formal submissions and have made a particular effort to engage with the African Diaspora. We are enormously grateful to all these individuals and groups for their contributions.

'Our Common Interest', the full report of the Commission for Africa, was presented to the world on 11 March 2005 in simultaneous events in London and Addis Ababa. In this book we present our report in the form of its Argument and Recommendations. This is the basis of our call to action. Our full report is in two parts. The Argument you will find here is the first part. It is followed by our Recommendations. These elements of our report are designed as a succinct statement of our findings for everyone who has contributed to or taken an interest in our work.

We hope that after reading the Argument and Recommendations, readers may wish to know more about the second part of our report. This is the Analysis and Evidence, which lays out the substance and basis of our recommendations so these can be held up to public scrutiny. The full report is available in English and French on our website www.commissionforafrica.org and may also be ordered as a single volume from that website. Suggestions for interested readers on this and other further reading appear at the end of this book.

Our report is written for many audiences. We address ourselves to decision-makers in Africa who must now drive forward the programme of change they have set out. We address ourselves to the rich and powerful nations of the world, whose leaders meet as the G8 in Gleneagles in Scotland in July 2005 where they must take a strong lead for action of a different order. We address ourselves to the international community, which must commit to greater and faster action on the Millennium Development Goals at the United Nations in September – and must also act boldly at the World Trade Organisation talks in Hong Kong in December.

And we address ourselves to the people of Africa and the world as a whole. For it is they who must demand action. It is only their insistence which will determine whether their political leaders take strong and sustained action.

The measures we propose constitute a coherent package for Africa. They must be delivered together. 2005 is the year to take the decisions that will show we are serious about turning the vision of a strong and prosperous Africa into a reality.

Tony Blair (Chair)

Fola Adeola	Ji Peiding
K Y Amoako	William Kalema
Nancy Kassebaum Baker	Trevor Manuel
Hilary Benn	Benjamin Mkapa
Gordon Brown	Linah Mohohlo
Michel Camdessus	Tidjane Thiam
Bob Geldof	Anna Tibaijuka
Ralph Goodale	Meles Zenawi

April 2005

Chapter 1: The case for action

Xamul aay na, laajtewul a ko raw.
Not to know is bad. Not to wish to know is worse.
  West African Proverb

Batta li a ifi ise agoura li arin egun.
With shoes, one can walk on thorns.
  West African Proverb

The world is awash with wealth, and on a scale which has never been seen before in human history. Unlike the opulence of the past, which belonged to a handful of privileged individuals and elites, this wealth is shared by unprecedented numbers of ordinary people across the planet. Growth and globalisation have brought higher living standards to billions of men and women.

Yet it is not a wealth which everyone enjoys. In Africa millions of people live each day in abject poverty and squalor. Children are hungry, their bodies stunted and deformed by malnutrition. They cannot read or write. They are needlessly ill. They have to drink dirty water. Those living in Africa's mushrooming shanty towns live by stinking rubbish tips and breathe polluted air.

We live in a world where new medicines and

medical techniques have eradicated many of the diseases and ailments which plagued the rich world. Yet in Africa some four million children under the age of five die each year, two-thirds of them from illnesses which cost very little to treat: malaria is the biggest single killer of African children, and half those deaths could be avoided if their parents had access to diagnosis and drugs that cost not much more than US$1 a dose.

We live in a world where scientists can map the human genome and have developed the technology even to clone a human being. Yet in Africa we allow more than 250,000 women to die each year from complications in pregnancy or childbirth.

We live in a world where the internet in the blink of an eye can transfer more information than any human brain could hold. Yet in Africa each day some 40 million children are not able to go to school.

We live in a world which, faced by one of the most devastating diseases ever seen, AIDS, has developed the anti-retroviral drugs to control its advance. Yet in Africa, where 25 million people are infected, those drugs are not made generally available. That means two million people will die of AIDS this year. In Zambia, by 2010 every third child will be an orphan.

We live in a world where rich nations spend as much as the entire income of all the people in Africa subsidising the unnecessary production of unwanted food – to the tune of almost US$1 billion a day. While in Africa hunger is a key factor in more deaths than all the continent's infectious diseases put together.

We live in a world where every cow in Europe has received almost US$2 a day in subsidies – double, grotesquely, the average income in Africa. And Japanese cows nearly US$4.

The contrast between the lives led by those who live in rich countries and poor people in Africa is the greatest scandal of our age. To convey the enormity of that injustice we speak in millions – and yet we have to remember that behind each statistic lies a child who is precious and loved. Every day that child, and thousands like her, will struggle for breath – and for life – and tragically and painfully lose that fight.

Globalisation must also mean justice on a global scale. The people of the world have an instinctive urge to help those in distress. The response to the tsunami which devastated the rim of the Indian Ocean showed that. More than 300,000 died when the most devastating earthquake of modern times sent a gigantic wave across the seas, destroying everything in its path when it hit the shore. It was an event of peculiarly dramatic horror and the people of the world reacted with spontaneous donations of cash on a scale which had never before been seen.

There is a tsunami every month in Africa. But its deadly tide of disease and hunger steals silently and secretly across the continent. It is not dramatic, and it rarely makes the television news. Its victims die quietly, out of sight, hidden in their pitiful homes. But they perish in the same numbers.

The eyes of the world may be averted from their routine suffering, but the eyes of history are upon us. In years to come, future generations will look back, and wonder how could our world have known and failed to act?

Everyone knows what Africa needs . . .

When the British Prime Minister, Tony Blair, launched this Commission many people responded: 'Why do we need a Commission? Surely everyone knows what Africa needs!' So we asked people to tell us. We held consultations across Africa and in the major cities of the rich world. We have examined the vast wealth of analysis of the last 50 years, and the mistakes which have been highlighted in aid, development and economic management. As a result we are now in a much better position to say what works and what does not, and to learn from those past failures and successes. Our report is evidence-based and pragmatic, with proposals which are based on sound analytical and practical arguments and evidence.

We have also done our best to be blisteringly honest. We write as 17 Commissioners, the majority of whom are Africans, but who include individuals from some of the world's richest countries, and we have done our best to face up to unpalatable truths wherever we have found them.

We have been frank about corruption, incompetence and conflict in Africa. And we have been direct in our criticisms of developed nations. Their trade policies are skewed to benefit the rich without consideration for the poor. They have been historically reluctant to lift the onerous debts which add to Africa's daily burden. And their aid policies have often seemed designed to support the political and industrial interests of the rich countries as much as to reduce poverty in Africa. Too much of the history of the industrialised world's involvement in Africa is a miserable history of broken promises.

It is not all a story of blame. We also address the natural disadvantages which are the legacy of Africa's geography, climate and history, and look at what both Africa and the industrialised world can do to help overcome that. And we have also taken into consideration the huge changes in the world's economy and politics which have taken place in the two decades since the Ethiopian famine of 1984/5, when Live Aid broadcast pictures of famine, death and poverty to a staggering 98 per cent of the world's television sets. Those images fixed the world in its view of Africa as a place of despair and dependency. But, though such scenes still exist, as a norm they are increasingly outdated. Things have changed significantly in the intervening 20 years, both in Africa and in the wider world.

For a start the Cold War is over and with it the superpowers' tendency to back corrupt dictators who manipulated Africa's wealth with no thought for economic development or the continent's poorest people – and reinforced the view that aid is commonly wasted or does not work. In South Africa, apartheid has crumbled, a transformation which has brought a new confidence to the whole of the continent. The end of apartheid has reminded Africa, and the world, that no injustice can last for ever. More darkly, the events in New York and Washington on September 11th 2001 have caused many in the rich world to reflect on the relationship between global poverty and homeland security. What happens to the poorest citizen in the poorest country can directly affect the richest citizen in the richest country. 'If a free society cannot help the many who are poor,' as the US President John F Kennedy once said, 'it cannot save the few who are rich'. Take all that together and this document becomes a declaration of our common interest.

Now more than ever we rely on each other not just for our sustenance but for our safety and security. As President George W Bush has said: 'Persistent poverty and oppression can lead to hopelessness and despair. And when governments fail to meet the most basic needs of their people, these failed states can become havens for terror . . . in many states around the world, poverty prevents governments from controlling their borders, policing their territory, and enforcing their laws. Development provides the resources to build hope and prosperity, and security.' Today the fortunes of the richest people in the richest countries are tied irrevocably to the fate of the poorest people in the poorest countries of the world, even though they are strangers and will never meet.

Nor are the changes over. Shifts in patterns of oil production and consumption mean that the United States is poised to take as much as 25 per cent of its oil from Africa within the next 10 years. On the world stage, Asia – and particularly the giants of China and India – is emerging as a major economic power. Chinese investments and business interests, for example, are now to be found all across Africa. In different parts of the globe the industrial age has been in many respects leap-frogged by the information revolution, the complete implications of which the world has yet to fully comprehend. All of this means that the time is ripe to look again at the part which the developed world can play in assisting Africa in its development.

We try in this report to tell a story. It is inevitably a complex story, for many of the issues impact on one another and cannot sensibly be addressed in isolation. The path we pick through this thicket of interactions is this. We begin by telling the world how the problem looks through African eyes, for the cultures of the continent are all too easily brushed aside in the rush to offer pre-packaged solutions from the developed world. Then we look at how Africa has to change in the areas of governance and peace and security, and how the industrialised world must change its behaviour too. We look at what is needed to help people, most particularly their health and education, and how to make sure that the poorest people are included in the economy and society. We consider the central issue of how to make African economies grow and, again, how to ensure that poor people can participate in, and benefit from, that growth; policy-makers must always consider the impact of policies on poor people. Then we look at trade, to discover what are the impediments to Africa selling more abroad, and how these can be removed. Then we look at the relationships between Africa and the rich world, in terms of trade, aid and debt — and how donors must change the way they do their business in Africa. In each of these areas we make specific recommendations, which are introduced here and spelled out in more detail in Part Two of our report. We conclude by turning our attention to how we can make our recommendations really happen – and monitor that they are properly implemented.

In all this we insist on the need for Africa's voice to be heard more clearly. And we underscore that the first responsibility for change and improved governance lies with Africans themselves, in which the rich world has a moral duty – as well as a powerful motive of self-interest – to assist.

Something new out of Africa

Our starting point is to tell the truth about Africa. That means we must point to successes as well as failures. In one African country after another the first signs are emerging that things may be changing. Twenty years ago it was commonplace for African countries to be run as dictatorships; today such governments are a minority. Democracy has new life. In the past five years, more than two-thirds of the countries in sub-Saharan Africa have had multi-party elections – some freer and fairer than others – with a number of examples of peaceful democratic changes of government. War has given way to peace in many places.

Where change has occurred a new generation of political leaders is emerging, many of whom voice a new commitment to the common good of the people. They seem set on reforming Africa's institutions too. The old Organisation for African Unity, with its policy of 'non-interference' in the internal affairs of other African states, has been transformed into the much stronger African Union which has a policy of 'non-indifference' to the suffering of the citizens in neighbouring countries who do not respect democracy, human rights and the need for peace. They have set up, as an arm of the African Union, a programme entitled the New Partnership for Africa's Development (NEPAD), which sees better government as an essential prerequisite of Africa's development. They have adopted an African Peer Review Mechanism to discover what policies and government systems have been shown to be most effective elsewhere. All these initiatives and bodies have still to prove their worth, but the first signs are encouraging. Backing now from the international community could make the difference on whether they succeed or fail.

In Africa, as elsewhere, there is a powerful link between political and economic development. Despite three decades of overall continental stagnation, growth exceeded 5 per cent in 24 separate countries in sub-Saharan Africa in 2003. A new entrepreneurship is in evidence and in several countries there is a growing middle class. A rich variety of pressure groups and community organisations are beginning to change the world around them and learning how to hold their governments to account. Also striking is the role of Africans living in the developed world. The flow of cash back home to Africa from relatives abroad is still low, compared with other developing regions, but it has increased dramatically in recent years. Everywhere there are the first signs of what could be a real momentum for change.

Of course, there are still oppressive regimes in

Africa. Corruption remains pervasive. Violent conflict is all too frequent. Inefficiency and waste and unnecessary bureaucracy are commonplace. Many nations lack the administrative and organisational capacity to deliver what their citizens require and deserve. But there is a new optimism abroad. More than half of the Africans interviewed by the polling organisation Afrobarometer expect their national economy to get 'better' or 'much better' in the year ahead. And the BBC World Service's Pulse of Africa survey found that in nearly every country at least 9 in 10 are proud to be African. There is also an increasing recognition that the responsibility to tackle all this lies squarely with Africans themselves. As the African winner of the Nobel Peace Prize, Wangari Maathai, said in her acceptance speech in December 2004:

Let us . . . intensify our commitment to our people, to reduce conflicts and poverty and thereby improve their quality of life. Let us embrace democratic governance, protect human rights and protect our environment. I am confident we shall rise to the occasion. I have always believed that solutions to most of our problems must come from us.

It is changes on the ground, like these, which have inspired us as Commissioners with the conviction that a singular moment has arrived for Africa. The challenge, for both Africans and their partners among developed nations, is to seize the new opportunity which change on the ground presents. Africa is at a crossroads. The path to the future for many African countries could drop inexorably down. Or it could continue the long slow climb to a better place. What we hope our report offers is a chart which will help take Africa on the upward path. But to follow it will require bold decisions from Africans and supportive action from the rest of the world.

Chapter 2: The lost decades

When the sun began to set on Europe's foreign empires, and former colonies across the globe began in the 1960s to prepare themselves for independence, nobody was that worried about Africa. The anxiety was all for Asia. After all Africa was a place of great mineral riches and vast agricultural fecundity. Asia, by contrast, seemed to have only problems and population. All the doomsday scenarios were centred in India and points east.

That was barely four decades ago. Today Africa is the poorest region in the world. Half of the population live on less than one dollar a day. Life expectancy is actually falling. People live, on average, to the age of just 46. In India and Bangladesh, by contrast, that figure is now a staggering 17 years higher.

Comparisons between Africa and Asia are revealing. For 30 years ago the average income in sub-Saharan Africa was twice that of both South and East Asia. In the intervening decades an astonishing turnaround has taken place. The average income in Africa is now well below half of that in East Asia. The story is similar in South Asia, Latin America and the Middle East. Africa is the only continent in the world which is stagnating. Why has Africa fallen so far behind?

In one sense its blessings proved also to be a curse. For the history of the past four decades reveals that the countries with the most oil, diamonds and other high-value natural resources are among those which have experienced the most war and armed conflict. Conflict is one of Africa's classic vicious circles. There can be no development without peace, but there can be no peace without development.

But Africa's great wealth provided it with a more systemic problem. The railways and roads put in place in colonial times were primarily designed to transport minerals and other raw materials from the African interior to its ports for shipping to Europe. They were not designed to join one part of the continent to another or generate more links to the East. Setting a map of African railways alongside those of India is very revealing: India's railways link the sub-continent; Africa's merely link areas of extraction to the ports. Today Africa's transport costs – local, national, or international – are today around twice as high as those for a typical Asian country. Shipping a car from Japan to Abidjan costs US$1,500, whereas moving it from Abidjan to Addis Ababa costs US$5,000.

The colonial era brought other problems. The division of Africa into its present countries was the product of Western interests not African minds. The lines drawn on a map by the great European powers in Berlin in 1884 still have profoundly disruptive consequences. Many traditional communities of people are now divided between two, three or even four countries. Elsewhere disparate groups, some of whom were traditional enemies, are yoked together in uneasy union, many of them lacking a common language with which to speak to one another.

Colonialism favoured some groups over others, creating new hierarchies. The consequences of some of these divisions are alive today, as was all too readily shown in Rwanda in the relationship between Hutu and Tutsi whose 'ethnic' differences were sharpened artificially during the colonial era, with such terrible consequences in the genocide of 1994.

'Let them each have a big mountain,' Queen Victoria is reported to have loftily pronounced when considering the division of land between what is now Kenya and Tanzania. The result is that many modern African states lack any natural geographic, ethnic, political or economic coherence. By contrast to the Indian sub-continent, where an effective administrative system was established, Africa was poorly served. Africa emerged from the colonial era with far weaker governance structures and infrastructure than other ex-colonies. Political borders have become economic barriers.

The legacy of all this is that Africa had a very weak starting point in the race for development. Even so in the 1960s, in the early years following independence, average incomes in Africa grew. It is no coincidence that, when the problems of the 1970s set in, the income of the average African declined. In that decade Africa became one of the battlegrounds on which the proxy conflicts of the Cold War were fought. Both sides backed venal despots who were less interested in developing their national economies than in looting the assets of the countries they ran and then stashed away billions of US dollars in their private Swiss bank accounts.

That decade only reinforced Africa's problems. While South Asia was busy expanding the area of land under irrigation, Africa's proportion of irrigated land hardly changed; over the last 20 years it has remained at around four per cent whilst South Asia's has risen to 40 per cent. Asia invested in rural roads and power, new crops, and science and technology. Africa fell behind there too.

One of the key failures of this period was not beginning to diversify African economies away from reliance on their key primary commodities. Today most African countries still rely on a very narrow range of exports. This leaves them highly vulnerable to long-term decline in the price of what they sell and to wild fluctuations in the world price of such commodities. From 1980 to 2000, the price of sugar fell by 77 per cent, cocoa by 71 per cent, coffee by 64 per cent and cotton by 47 per cent. Africa's export prices are nearly four times more volatile than those of developed countries.

Again comparisons with Asia are greatly to Africa's disadvantage. The last 20 years has seen a huge change in developing countries. The proportion of manufactured goods in their exports has risen from just 20 per cent to a staggering 80 per cent. Asia has led the way. It has developed the industrial infrastructure, skills and learning culture which Africa lacks. The task of breaking into new markets is now harder for Africa than ever before. Another vicious circle.

All this has had a knock-on effect. Investors, both domestic and foreign, see Africa as an undifferentiated whole – war in one country casts long shadows not just over neighbouring states but over the whole continent. As a result Africa seems to many outsiders an unattractive place in which to invest or keep their money. And what money is made in Africa is encouraged to flow out. Around 40 per cent of African savings are kept outside the continent, compared with just six per cent for East Asia and three per cent for South Asia. What is true of money is also true of people. Many educated Africans have over the years quit their homelands because they are frustrated at not being able to put their skills to good use. They can also earn more and have a better life elsewhere. Africa loses an average of 70,000 skilled personnel a year to developed countries in this brain drain. Zambia has lost all but 400 of its 1,600 doctors in recent years.

A healthy and skilled workforce is vital to the success of any economic activity. Healthcare and education are the birthrights of every child but they are also essential for the health of the nation. Countries cannot develop properly if only elites are educated. Countries with poor health and low levels of education find it more difficult to achieve economic growth.

Here again Africa's record on human development is poor compared to that of East and South Asia. The decades in which Asia was investing, the 1970s and 1980s, were the years of crisis when African governments were slashing the budgets of both clinics and schools at the behest of the International Monetary Fund. Evidence shows that IMF and World Bank economic policy in the 1980s and early 1990s took little account of how these policies would potentially impact on poor people in Africa. Many health and education systems began to break down. And all of this came just as AIDS began to take its deadly toll. This illustrates another of the vicious circles so typical of poverty traps. Without functioning clinics and schools a healthy and skilled workforce is harder to achieve; without such a workforce one of the key conditions for creating economic growth is removed; without economic growth there is no money to invest in clinics and schools.

Africa's problem is that all these vicious circles inter-lock. That is why tackling them requires strong action in all these areas at the same time.

Africa's relationship with the rich world

Three sometimes contradictory dynamics dominate the relationship between Africa and the industrialised nations: they involve trade, debt and aid. In the last few decades, Africa has seen its share of world trade fall from six per cent in 1980 to less than two per cent in 2002. The industrialised world has been unhelpful here. Indeed it has been a wilful obstacle. The European Union, Japan, the United States and many other rich countries all heavily subsidise their agriculture, which then depresses world prices in the subsidised commodities. Local farmers then find that they can-not produce crops at prices which compete with products so heavily funded by taxpayers in G8 nations. Poor countries have complained to the World Trade Organisation about this and had their complaints upheld. But reform of the EU's Common Agricultural

Policy and US farm policy is painfully slow. Indeed the amount the developed world spent just subsidising its agriculture – much of which goes to big agribusiness – was in 2002 the equivalent of the income of all the people in sub-Saharan Africa put together.

That is far from the only problem with trade. Developed nations place taxes on goods exported to them; agricultural produce imported into Europe, for example, must pay an average tariff of 22 per cent. There is a whole variety of such barriers on products of interest to Africa; for instance, tariffs on peanuts coming into the US are 132 per cent. Some of these barriers have been reduced over the years but new barriers have been introduced. These indefensible trade barriers must go; though as we shall see, these are not the only impediment to trade for Africa. Finally, African economic policy relating to trade, such as moves to liberalise sectors of the economy, is too often a condition of receiving aid from donors. If they are to be accountable to their own citizens African governments have to be allowed the space to make their own decisions.

The second problematic area in the relationship between Africa and the developed world is that of debt. There is strong resentment in many parts of Africa over these debt obligations, in part because much of the debt was incurred by unelected leaders supported by the very countries now receiving money to cover the service of those debts – and who, many Africans feel, are now using debt as a lever to dictate policy to the continent. There is a widespread feeling that the debts are unreasonable and that what was owed has in practice already been paid many times over.

Over the years Africa has had difficulty in paying off the interest – let alone the capital – on these debts. Even after various rounds of debt reduction, sub-Saharan Africa still pays out more on debt service than it spends on health (around three per cent of its annual income). For every US$2 Africa currently receives in aid, it pays back nearly US$1 in debt payments.

The third key area in the relationship of Africa with the rich world is that of aid. In some quarters there is much scepticism about aid. It is seen as ineffective, stolen or wasted. There is no doubt that this has been the case in the past, for example in Mobutu's Zaire. There is also no doubt that some countries have not had the capacity to handle aid effectively. But the evidence on the effectiveness of aid, which we have examined very carefully, shows that it is simply untrue that aid to Africa has been wasted in more recent years.

Strong lessons have been learned and Africa is changing. But there are areas in which African governments must accelerate that change before extra aid can yield its full potential. In addition international donors must seriously improve the way aid is delivered. This report will recommend fundamental changes in the behaviour of African countries, rich countries and in the relationship between them.

The key issue of governance

One thing underlies all the difficulties caused by the interactions of Africa's history over the past 40 years. It is the weakness of governance and the absence of an effective state. By governance we mean the inability of government and the public services to create the right economic, social and legal framework which will encourage economic growth and allow poor people to participate in it. All the evidence shows that reductions in poverty do not come without economic growth. But as any gardener will testify, growth will not occur unless the right conditions are in place. Horticulturally that will be the right soil and temperature and water and light in appropriate amounts. Economically, since growth is driven principally by the private sector, that requires governments to provide a climate in which ordinary people – whether they be small farmers or managers of larger firms – can get on with their daily tasks untroubled, and feel that it is worthwhile investing in their future. That climate is what is consistently lacking right across Africa.

At the heart of the proper function of government is establishing an economic environment that encourages investment. That means basic functions such as providing security, setting sound economic policies under the law, collecting taxes and delivering adequate public services like health and education. It means seeing that physical infrastructure is in place – roads, railways, water, electricity and telecommunications. But there are also more abstract forms of infrastructure, such as legal systems to protect basic property rights, human rights, and respect for contracts, to uphold order and to act as a check on governments.

This function extends beyond the direct business of government into a wider area of governance. It is about ensuring that other institutions are in place: an independent judiciary, an effective impartial police and prison system, and a wide range of financial and regulatory systems such as central banks, land registries, and bodies to administer ports and customs posts. All these require skilled public servants and managers, at national and at local government level. And they in turn need training, as well as basic equipment such as the tools of keeping records, files, accounting systems, telephones and computers. Without all that the capacity of governments in the modern world to do their job is sorely constrained.

It is those governance systems, and the capacity to make them work, which Africa so badly lacks. And, to achieve that, government processes have to be properly open to scrutiny. Knowing what money has been received, and how it is meant to be spent, gives citizens the means to hold governments to account.

The issue of good governance and capacity-building is what we believe lies at the core of all of Africa's problems. Until that is in place Africa will be doomed to continue its economic stagnation.

Why now?

The long history of Africa's decline might lead some people to suggest that there can be no urgency about taking radical action. The opposite is the case. Africa cannot wait. The plan we set out here needs action now.

The most obvious reason for immediacy is that

across Africa people are needlessly dying every day. Deep levels of deprivation mean continued human suffering. Common human decency insists that delay cannot be an option.

But there are other reasons. We are storing up trouble for the future. The longer Africa's problems are left unaddressed the worse they will get. The contagion of AIDS will multiply if it is left unchecked. So too will diseases like tuberculosis, which spreads like the common cold and which is currently moving across the continent at the rate of one person per second. Poverty leads to actions for short-term survival, such as selling assets or cutting down trees, which often undermine conditions for future recovery. Irreversible damage is being done to the natural environment, threatening future food supplies.

The huge slum cities of Africa are growing apace, day by day, unplanned, and in ways which threaten serious social tensions in years to come. This chaotic urbanisation is a classic example of the costs of delay. The population of Africa is exploding. Some 37 per cent of Africans now live in cities and that figure will rise to more than 50 per cent over the next 20 years. On present trends Africa will be, by 2030, an urban continent. Already 166 million people live in slums. Living conditions there are made worse by the lack of access to water, sewage, electricity, refuse collection or other municipal services from local authorities ill-equipped, or unwilling, to address them. In cities like Nairobi 60 per cent of the people live on just five per cent of the land. And these slums are filled with an increasingly youthful population, unemployed and disaffected. Africa's cities are becoming a powder-keg of potential instability and discontent.

Yet, as with all these problems, early action can help to manage these trends. When girls are educated, when incomes rise, when reproductive healthcare is available, and when parents know that the rate of child mortality is falling, then birth rates slow. All these things can be comparatively rapidly achieved, as the history of Bangladesh and India has shown.

Inaction brings another danger. Those new African leaders who are committed to change have put in place reforms – on the economy and on combating corruption – that have been politically difficult. Those leaders could be evicted from office if their people do not see returns. That might mean some of the changes which are set to improve life in Africa in the medium to long term could be reversed. Other leaders might be deterred from venturing down that same path. That is why supportive action by the developed world is urgent.

Africa today has its best opportunity for change for decades. But the future is finely balanced. The rich world now has the chance to tip that balance towards the possibility of success and away from the likelihood of failure. The risks from delay far outweigh the risks of acting strongly and swiftly.

Chapter 3: Through African eyes

Ask the big question: 'What is development for?' and you get very different answers in different cultures. Many in Western countries see it as being about places like Africa 'catching up' with the developed world. In Africa, by contrast, you will be more likely to be told something to do with well-being, happiness and membership of a community. In the West development is about increasing choice for individuals; in Africa it is more about increasing human dignity within a community. Unless those who shape Africa's development make this integral to the way they formulate their policies they will fail.

The trouble is that in the debate on development, though we all use the same terms, we often don't mean the same thing by them. Different cultures manifest their ideas of political and economic freedom in very different ways. For this reason the Commission decided to consider the issue of culture before embarking on political and economic analysis. By culture we are talking about far more than literature, music, dance, art, sculpture, theatre, film and sport. All of these, of course, are for any social group part of its shared joy in the business of being alive. But culture is more than the arts. It is about shared patterns of identity. It is about how social values are transmitted and individuals are made to be part of a society.

Culture is how the past interacts with the future.

Africa's past is one in which, in pre-colonial times, people grouped themselves through clans. Their culture was strong on kinship ties and a sense that the members of the group were responsible for and to one another. Many of these features, such as the relationship between elders and non-elders, persist today. Not least here is the 'big man' culture which requires a successful member of the clan to offer patronage to other members – a phenomenon which is rarely taken with sufficient seriousness by development policymakers. Patron-client relations should not be dismissed as temptations to nepotism and corruption; they reveal something about African senses of community.

Culture in this sense is not some bolt-on extra. It has to be built into our understanding, our analysis and our process. That is one of the reasons why, from the outset, we insisted that the Commission for Africa must consult as widely as possible, within Africa as well as within the developed world. As one of our Commissioners, Trevor Manuel, South Africa's finance minister, put it, quoting an African proverb: 'Until the lions have spoken the only history will be that of the hunters.' The consultation we launched had participants who ranged from east African slum dwellers and women from rural West Africa to the top elected and unelected decision-makers in Africa and the rich world. We asked them all the same question: what is actually working across the continent, and what is not?

Time and again two messages were reinforced to us. The first was of the need to recognise Africa's huge diversity. The second largest continent in the world, it contains more than 50 countries which hold an enormously rich mix of peoples, cultures, economies, history and geographies. Africa is many places, as is reflected in the French expression 'les Afriques'. This means that there can be no 'one size fits all' solutions.

The second message was that Africa's strength lies in social networks which are invisible to many outsiders. What can appear to donors as a form of anarchy is in fact structured; it is just that these are structures which Westerners are not trained to perceive. Africans survive – and some prosper – in the face of low incomes and few jobs in the formal economy. They do so using a complex network of social relations that make decisions about who gets start-up capital for small enterprises or interest-free loans in emergencies. These networks may be informal but they reveal how African people will get involved in activities where they can see purpose and direction.

What is also clear is that, in many places, such networks are seen as alternatives to the state. That is most obviously true in places like Somalia where the state has completely collapsed. But all across Africa there are 'failed states' in the sense that they are unable to provide the basic legal and economic frameworks, or public services like health and education, which citizens expect. There is a widespread cynicism with politicians. In the Wolof language the word *politig* has come to mean lying or deception. Voters have become disillusioned. Turnout is in decline in elections all across Africa.

For too many, perhaps a majority, the state is an irrelevance or a burden. For them their primary loyalty remains with the family, clan or tribe. Increasingly, though, something else is moving into the vacuum. It is religion. Religion has always been important in Africa but at present all across Africa people are converting in large numbers to Christianity, often in its more evangelical manifestations, and to Islam, most particularly in the puritan Wahhabi form, encouraged by money from Saudi Arabia. There is also a big revival in traditional African religions, including secret initiation societies. Where the state can no longer deliver, religious movements are gaining a new attractiveness.

This has very practical consequences. In the Congo, because there is no working national postal service, people leave letters in Catholic churches to be transmitted to other parts of the Congo since the Church is the only reasonably coherent nationwide infrastructure. In Senegal the Mouride Brotherhood has expanded to cover almost a third of the population with a singular mixture of Sufi Islam, entrepreneurial enthusiasm and committed members overseas who remit significant amounts of money. Religion, particularly Islam and Christianity, offers a way to plug into globalisation. Saudi Arabia and Persian Gulf countries have become part of an African trading network as well as reception zones for African migrant workers. And many of the new evangelical churches have relationships with rich churches in the United States.

This has at least two implications for development in Africa. Religion can be a model for the state. If the African state is to become more effective it needs to understand what it is about religion that builds loyalty, creates infrastructure, collects tithes and taxes, fosters a sense that it delivers material as well as spiritual benefits. Religion can, of course, be misused but it can also be a partner in development. Faith leaders have great influence on shaping social attitudes, community relationships, personal responsibility and sexual morals. In Ethiopia the government recently secured a ruling from the Patriarch of the Ethiopian Orthodox Church which gave farmers permission to work on 160 days a year which had previously been thought of as religious festivals, when to work would be a sin; agricultural productivity has since risen by more than 20 per cent a year. In Kenya medical workers are already using shamans to transmit primary healthcare. Clerics, traditional religious leaders and Islamic imams are increasingly prominent in the fight against HIV and AIDS. But this must not be seen simply as an attempt to co-opt religious leaders and traditional healers into disseminating the messages of foreign cultures. An appreciation of the role of religion in African life will require some fundamentally different approaches by the international community.

One commonly held fallacy about culture is that it is the expression of unchanging tradition. Those who hold this view usually see African cultures as regressive and tribal and therefore inimical to development. African culture, they often say, is an irrational force that generates inertia and economic backwardness. This is contrary to the evidence. History shows African cultures to have been tremendously adaptive, absorbing a wide range of outside influences, and impositions, as well finding ways to survive often difficult natural, environmental and social conditions. Such influences are not all positive. Many African cultures nurture a sense of denial and passivity, or encourage the abuse of women, or pay respect to the elderly with such deference that they exclude the young who now make up half the population of the continent. But the dynamics of culture mean that people can be critical of what they have inherited. The lesson is that culture is an agent of economic and social change.

The way that the mobile phone is changing life in Africa today is a vivid example of that. The use of mobile phones in Africa is increasing much faster than anywhere else in the world. Some 75 per cent of all telephones in Africa are mobile. A driving force in their spread has been the need for people to keep in touch with family news, but cellphones are also used to help poor people in remote areas find employment without travelling long distances. But the new technology is bringing many indirect spin-offs.

In farming communities in Tanzania, where butchers cannot stock large amounts of meat because they have no electricity or cannot afford a refrigerator, shops previously often ran out of meat. Nowadays customers use mobiles to place orders ahead of collection, enabling butchers to buy the right amount to satisfy their customers' needs and developing the entire supply chain. Mobile servers on motorbikes are now providing telephone connections in rural parts of South Africa. Already evidence is emerging that data collection via cellphones has the potential to dramatically increase efficiency within health budgets; pilot schemes in Uganda are already showing savings of as much as 40 per cent.

The continent is ahead of much of the world in the use of prepaid phone cards as a form of electronic currency. Africans in the developed world are buying prepaid cards and sending them, via cellphones, to their relatives back home, who can then sell the cards to others. Thus the cards have become a form of currency by which money can be sent from the rich world to Africa without incurring the commission charged on more conventional ways of remitting money.

The mobile phone is creating virtual infrastructures and raising the possibility of unthought-of transformations in African culture, infrastructure and politics: studies show that when 20 per cent of a population has the ability to exchange news and ideas through access to cellphones and text messaging, dictatorial or totalitarian regimes find it hard to retain power. Changes such as these should alert us to the possibility of other developments which it is difficult if not impossible to foresee – and which may undermine some of the traditional assumptions in our thinking about development. A report like this must always leave room for us to expect the unexpected.

Those who ignore culture are doomed to failure in Africa. The outsiders who ran a workshop on AIDS in Angola recently learned that. They came to pass on their knowledge about transmission and prevention. They left having obtained new understandings of cultural practices such as initiation rites, scar-tattooing, blood brother practices, means of breaking the umbilical cord, polygamy and traditional marriage and healing practices. Only then did they come to understand why their education and awareness programmes had not resulted in higher use of condoms or lowered rates of infection. They had not known enough about local cultural norms and values on sexuality.

Those who understand culture can find new ways to succeed. Before civil war plunged Somalia into a condition of warlord-dominated anarchy, order was maintained by the country's traditional courts of tribal elders, the Tol. These made each clan collectively responsible for the actions of its individual members – if one man stole, his whole clan could be fined for it. In most parts of the country the power of the Tol has been abolished by the warlords. But in Somaliland, a place of modest but ordered prosperity, the Tol has not only been retained: it has been incorporated into the second chamber of parliament. Few in Somaliland doubt that the continued existence of the old system is a key component in the relative stability there. Such a hybrid system is not one which a political theorist might have invented given a blank sheet of paper. But it is one, with its odd mix of African and Western systems of governance, that clearly works. The challenge is to harness the cultures of Africa to find such workable hybrids for the rest of the continent.

The overall lesson is that outside prescriptions only succeed where they work with the grain of African ways of doing things. They fail where they ignore, or do not understand, the cultural suppositions of the people they seek to address. The international community must make greater efforts to understand the values, norms and allegiances of the cultures of Africa and in their policy-making display a greater flexibility, open-mindedness and humility.

Chapter 4: Getting systems right: governance and capacity-building

A cornerstone of development is a state with a sound constitution that balances the interest of all its citizens, and that separates powers of the judiciary and legislature from the executive. This provides the framework within which the private sector can create the economic growth without which the lives of poor people can never be substantially improved. That means a state which has the ability to maintain peace and security and protect the freedom and human rights of its citizens, to design policies that will enable ordinary people to build a better life, and to deliver the public services its citizens require.

There is more to governance than how the government conducts itself. It is about the whole realm in which the state operates, including areas like parliament, the judiciary, the media and all the other organisations of society which remain in place when a government changes. Next it is about the policies of government. But it is also about whether a government has the staff and organisational systems to design its policies and the ability to implement them with the participation of its citizens.

It also has another crucial dimension: how well the government answers to its people for its policies and actions, whether it is 'accountable' to its citizens. Democracy of some kind is an absolute fundamental here. But this is about much more than elections every five years to allow for a change of leaders. Many Africans call into question the legitimacy of the constitutions of their states, in which the balance between the executive, parliament and the judiciary shifted to the executive at independence and paved the way for the one-party state in the years that followed. Other leaders ignore constitutions and stay in power longer than is constitutionally permitted. Africans need to address these issues, and developed nations should offer technical and financial support.

More prosaically, for accountability to be effective, a government's policies, actions and systems need to be open to scrutiny by its people. This openness is not just a question of attitude; it has to be woven into the very systems through which the state operates.

Fortunately there is an increasing recognition of all this among African governments. They are now working more closely together, through the African Union, to tackle this. Some 24 countries, representing 75 per cent of Africa's population, have so far signed up to an initiative by the African Union's NEPAD programme to establish an African Peer Review Mechanism where a country puts itself forward for scrutiny by its peers to help identify its weaknesses and the actions needed to correct them. The aim is to foster adoption of good policies and practice by sharing information on what is working, and what is not. Peer pressure produces a strong incentive to act. The initiative is in its early days but its first actions have been promising and this Commission recommends that rich countries support it. For a relatively small amount of money this mechanism could lever significant change. Details on this, as on all our recommendations, are given in Part Two of this report.

The capacity to deliver

Good governance is about much more than sound policies. Governments have to be able to put those policies into effect. A number of practical factors constrain African states' capacity to do this. Africa has had insufficient money to invest in technology, health and education systems, roads, power grids, telecoms, affordable housing and water supply and sanitation. It has poor quality systems for the collection of data, without which government policies can neither be properly formulated nor accurately monitored. Its civil servants, in national and local government, often do not have the training to analyse complex information or plan and budget effectively. Quality of management and incentive systems have been poor. Public servants are also being hit by AIDS. In Zambia teachers are dying faster than they can be trained.

International donors have in recent years tried to invest in building this capacity – the ability to design and deliver services. But results have been patchy. We have looked at the reasons for this. Reforms have been piecemeal, rather than part of a wider strategy. African governments have not been fully committed to them. And donors supplied assistance in ways which were counter-productive. Instead of strengthening the abilities of African ministries, donors created Project

Implementation Units to run individual projects. In the short term these may have worked, but in the longer term getting outsiders to 'do the job' does nothing to improve the skills of the civil servants.

An entirely different approach is required. Strong backing is now being given by most African countries to the African Union's NEPAD programme which puts new emphasis on strengthening institutions. The starting point must be comprehensive strategies drawn up by African governments to build capacity throughout their administrations. The international community should support these strategies, and make sure that the aid efforts of individual donor nations do not undermine them. This improved capacity needs to be built in national ministries and also at local government level, but it is also needed at a continental level in the African Union and in the various regional economic communities through which countries work together.

Transforming bureaucracies will not be achieved overnight. Donors must recognise that in most African countries change will be long, slow and complicated. That means rich countries must provide assistance in a way that allows African governments to plan over a longer term than at present. Without a long-term predictable flow of funds which can be used for salaries or maintenance, governments will be reluctant to build schools or hire teachers. Donors must also guard against poaching the most talented civil service staff, and thus weakening the structure still further. And African governments should address weak management, lack of incentives for individuals to get things right and poor motivation which are often more critical. So is the need to attract, motivate and retain skilled staff. A survey in Malawi showed that 25 per cent of teachers who started work in rural areas in January 1999 had left by October that same year.

The shortage of skilled professionals in Africa is a critical issue. It has its roots in a tertiary education system that is in a state of crisis. The emphasis in Africa in recent years has rightly been on the need for primary education. An unfortunate side-effect of this has been the neglect of secondary and tertiary education from which are produced the doctors, nurses, teachers, police officers, lawyers and government workers of tomorrow. Africa's universities ought to be the breeding ground for the skilled individuals whom the continent needs. There is a particular shortage in the science skills that are fundamental to addressing Africa's problems. Africa needs higher education and research institutes that attract students, researchers and teachers to study and work in Africa – at present there are more African scientists and engineers working in the USA than in Africa. A long-term programme of investment is needed, both to revitalise African universities and to support the development of centres of excellence in science, engineering and technology, including African institutes of technology.

Answering to the people – accountability

There is another key condition that is required for good governance. It is accountability – by which we mean a system which ensures that governments are

answerable to their people for the way they run the
country. Too often in the past African governments have responded not to the interests of all their
people but to those of elites, parties, tribes or other
particular groups. Sometimes they have even put the
demands of the international donor community before
the concerns of their citizens.

Governments must be answerable to all their people,
including the poorest and most vulnerable. Clearly
they are not felt to do this at present. The Globescan
survey commissioned by this Commission reveals
that for most Africans, the primary responsibility
for creating the problems in their country is laid at
the door of their national governments: 49 per cent of
those surveyed blamed their own politicians – three
times more than blamed the formal colonial powers,
16 per cent, or rich countries, just 11 per cent.

The answer to this is putting mechanisms in place
to make sure that the voices of all citizens can actually
influence decisions of their governments. To do this
requires good economic and financial management
systems. But it also means empowering key groups
within society. African parliamentarians need training
and mentoring – for their work in their national
parliaments and also in the nascent Pan-African parliament – from their counterparts in other developing
countries with strong parliaments and in the developed
world. They also need a greater representation of
women. Africa's system of justice – which has a vital
role in enforcing human rights, contracts and property
rights, and acting as a check on government – needs
strengthening. African governments could do this by a

host of measures including guaranteeing tenure for judges, introducing computerised case management and bolstering democratic mechanisms to oversee the judiciary. Judges from more developed countries could also assist here.

Likewise with the media. Africa's journalists have a crucial role in holding the government to account and exposing corruption and inefficiency. But at present its journalists are not sufficiently free or professional. They need more training, in both journalistic techniques and professional ethics. African governments can assist media independence by granting commercial licences for radio stations to compete with the state-owned stations from which most Africans get their news. Journalists and editors in other countries could assist here too.

Developed countries can also support the strengthening of another crucial sector which has the power to hold governments responsible for their actions. The organisations of civil society – trade associations, farmers' organisations, business groups, trades unions, development agencies, women's organisations, faith groups and community groups – all have a role to play in ensuring that those in charge truly reflect what the various sections of society want. The number of these civil society organisations has risen dramatically over the last decade or so, but many of them require help to develop the skills they need to spot dubious priorities, conflicts of interest or a lack of probity in public finances. Again their counterparts in other developing and developed nations could help.

Corruption and transparency

For political leaders to be held accountable, citizens must have proper information about government revenues and budget allocations. Openness makes it more likely that resources will be used efficiently. By contrast a lack of transparency encourages corruption, especially where politicians and officials are members of secret societies, which are common in Africa as in the rest of the world. This lack of openness is a particular problem where income – particularly that derived from oil, minerals and other high-value natural resources – is managed in a way which hides accounts from the public.

Corruption is systemic in much of Africa today. It is another of Africa's vicious circles: corruption has a corrosive effect on efforts to improve governance, yet improved governance is essential to reduce the scope for corruption in the first place. All this harms the poorest people in particular because it diverts funds away from providing the services they need more than anyone else in society and they are likely to have to pay a higher percentage of their income in bribes. Africa has begun to tackle this. Its politicians have agreed through the African Peer Review Mechanism to assess their performance against a number of internationally-agreed codes and standards, including those on fiscal and monetary transparency. They now need to adapt these to the African context because many of them have been designed for countries which are already far more developed than Africa and which have different capabilities and face different economic policy challenges.

The rot of corruption has spread throughout society at all levels. But to send a strong signal it is worth tackling the most egregious examples. The international community can assist in two ways. First, it should track down money looted by corrupt African leaders, now sitting in foreign bank accounts, and send that money back to the states from whom it was stolen. This will send out a clear message to current and future leaders that they will not be allowed to profit from such immoral behaviour. Second, rich nations should put in place a series of measures to make theft of national assets more difficult and to deter their own companies from paying bribes in the first place. After all as the former Zairean dictator President Mobutu Sese Seko once reputedly said: 'It takes two to be corrupt – the corrupted and the corrupter.' And he should know.

We are talking huge sums here. It is estimated that the amount stolen, and now held in foreign bank accounts, is equivalent to more than half of the continent's external debt. In the worst cases, the amounts held by individuals in foreign bank accounts run into billions of US dollars. Developed countries must require banks within their jurisdiction to inform on such deposits and to repatriate them to the proper authorities. Action is needed in five linked areas:

Prevention: Measures are required to prevent the theft of assets in the first place. Appropriate offences must be put on

African statute books. Each nation's financial institutions must have anti-money-laundering controls in place.

Identification: Systems must be improved so it is possible to recognise when funds in an account have been acquired illicitly. Rich countries have developed advanced money-laundering controls in the war on terror and drugs which can be used here. Banks should be obliged to inform African states where they see suspicious transactions.

Freezing: Laws must be changed to make easier the freezing of assets at a much earlier stage in a criminal investigation, preventing money from being moved while further investigations are carried out.

Confiscation: Mechanisms should be established to enable the confiscation of assets without the necessity for criminal conviction. All developed country governments should introduce laws to make confiscation possible without the necessity for a criminal conviction and find ways to reduce the number of time-wasting appeals allowed in these cases.

Repatriation: The states in which the banks that hold the funds are located must create instruments for returning the funds to the state from which they were looted.

Rich nations should give technical assistance to help develop Africa's capacity in these areas.

But corruption goes far beyond the actions of a few kleptocratic leaders. It is present at all levels. What really matters to poor people is petty corruption. At the grassroots level that is a question of African governments demonstrating the political will for a crackdown on corruption. But there is much the international community could do. Attention must focus on the bribe-giver as well as the bribe-taker. Numerous international anti-bribery agreements exist already to curb corruption. They should be enforced more rigorously. The UN Convention Against Corruption – the first international legal instrument to recognise the need for all states to commit to asset repatriation – has not been ratified by one single member of the G8. It can come into force only if it is ratified by 30 states. It is pointless for the developed world to bemoan African corruption when it does not take the specific measures needed to counter it.

Transparency is especially important in countries rich in mineral wealth. All the evidence shows that oil, for example, usually enriches only the ruling elite. For the vast majority of the population mineral wealth often appears merely to increase corruption, poverty and political instability. African electorates need to demand that government books on revenues from mineral extraction are opened to public scrutiny.

The international community also has a role to play. As well as cracking down directly on bribery it can demand higher standards from multinational companies active in developing countries. Where there are no laws to govern the actions of foreign companies, codes and standards should be used to guide behaviour. Shareholders and consumers must exercise their considerable influence to ensure that such codes and standards are followed.

One promising initiative in this field is the Extractive Industries Transparency Initiative, which is being implemented in a number of African countries. Under it, oil, gas and mining companies publicly disclose all payments they make to governments, and governments, in turn, publish what they receive from these companies. Individual citizens and concerned groups can then scrutinise these. This scheme is in its early days, and work is still underway to clarify exactly what it means to implement the initiative. It may not solve all the problems immediately but it is an important first step towards greater accountability. The international community and more African governments need to back this initiative and encourage all resource-rich countries to sign up to it, as Nigeria, Ghana, Republic of Congo and São Tomé e Principe have already done. That includes funding the training of civil servants, and public systems to make the scheme work. The civil society organisations who monitor it will also need similar assistance. But the oil and mining sectors are not the only ones where money is lost due to poor management and corruption. Sectors like the forestry and fisheries industries could also benefit from more openness about revenue flows, and the international community should support this.

One area that suffers particularly severely from corruption is procurement – the way that governments buy in goods and services. Abuse of this system takes many forms. When public sector contracts are put out to sealed tender, bribes – known by euphemisms such as 'signature bonuses' – can be requested or offered. Quotations can be doctored to build in false costs. It is not only the politicians and public officials who create the problem: it is also the bankers, lawyers,

accountants, and engineers working on public contracts. Widescale corruption adds at least 25 per cent
to the costs of government procurement, frequently
resulting in inferior quality construction and unnecessary purchases. A crackdown on all this is in the hands
of Africa's leaders, who must demonstrate the political
will to follow through what they have started. But
the international community can help here too. It must
encourage more transparent methods of selling goods
and services both in Africa and the developed world.
Rich countries' Export Credit Agencies – government-
backed bodies which provide loans, guarantees, credits
and insurance to private companies who invest or
engage in trade with developing countries – can make
their funds conditional on compliance with anti-
bribery measures.

These are the main measures required on governance. Unless there are improvements in all these
areas this Commission has concluded, after a detailed
review of all the evidence, that all the other reforms
we will recommend – in international trade, debt and
aid – will have only limited impact.

Chapter 5: The need for peace and security

Out of sight of the world, in the biggest death toll since the Second World War, around 1,000 people die every day in the Democratic Republic of Congo. It is only one of Africa's many conflicts. In recent decades Africa has experienced more brutal coups, drawn-out civil wars and bloody instability than any other part of the world. Some of this, like the violence in Darfur, has been high profile. But there are countless smaller conflicts, such as those between herders and cultivators which are to be found in many parts of Africa, which are no less vicious. Violence causes as many deaths in Africa as does disease.

The human cost of all this is devastating. Millions of lives have been lost. At least three million people died in four years in the civil war in the Democratic Republic of Congo alone. As a result of 'localised' conflict in Nigeria, for example, at least 10,000 people lost their lives between 1999 and 2003 and an estimated 800,000 were internally displaced. More people have been forced to flee their homes in Africa than anywhere else in the world, many ending up in the slums of already-overcrowded cities and towns. Malnutrition and disease increase. And those who suffer most are the poor and the vulnerable. War does not only harm people. It destroys roads, bridges, farming equipment, telecommunications, water and sanitation systems. It shuts down hospitals and schools. It slows trade and economic life, sometimes to a halt. The very fabric of society is torn asunder.

But conflict has a much wider consequence. Instability in Africa undermines global security. States weakened by strife increase international refugee flows. They also become havens for international terrorist organisations. In the face of all this it may seem odd to talk of optimism. But things are beginning to change in Africa. There is now hope of peace in many of Africa's most war-torn places such as Angola and Sierra Leone. There are even glimmers of hope in the Democratic Republic of Congo, Sudan and Somalia. Countries such as Mozambique, once previously synonymous with violence and suffering, have maintained peace for over a decade now. How do we continue this improvement?

Prevention is better than cure

Until now the international community's main focus has been on intervening in conflict – militarily or with humanitarian assistance. But this Commission has concluded that donors must place far more emphasis on building the foundations for durable human security and supporting African institutions in attempts to prevent the outbreak of fighting in the first place. This is for a number of reasons.

Once armed hostilities have begun they are difficult and costly to resolve – and create a higher risk of further violence in the future. Even after fighting is over the evidence is that nervous governments keep levels of military expenditure high. This means that resources are diverted away from rebuilding society in a way which tackles some of the social problems which may have contributed to the cause of fighting in the first place. Thus, countries that have experienced one civil war have an increased likelihood of further fighting within five years. Violent conflict is another of Africa's vicious circles.

The costs are also high for the international community. Donor nations respond to violent conflict, in the main, through deployment of peacekeepers and through development work once fighting is over. This is expensive. The budget for UN peacekeeping operations in Africa for the year to June 2005 is US$2.86 billion. On top of this is the cost of aid to war zones; Africa received around US$7 billion in humanitarian aid between 1995–2001. Much of this was in response to conflict.

War means rebuilding vital infrastructure. The cost of the material damage during the Rwandan genocide was around US$1 billion. Reconstruction for the Democratic Republic of Congo is estimated at US$20 billion and even if strong growth starts now it will take several decades for the country to get back to the level of per capita wealth it had at independence in 1960. A number of studies have shown that conflict prevention is much more cost-effective than intervention. One estimate is that it would have cost US$1.5 billion to prevent the outbreak of fighting in Somalia compared with the US$7.3 billion it cost to respond. Just 5,000 troops with robust peace enforcement capabilities could have saved half a million lives in Rwanda. Evidence shows that prevention can work.

So why has there not been more emphasis on prevention? Partly because of the 'CNN factor'. The high profile given to some emergencies by the media puts strong pressure on international politicians to respond to them – and provides political rewards for doing so. By contrast creating unglamorous mechanisms to address Africa's vulnerability to violence may not draw the headlines, but it is far more effective and far cheaper. The international community must invest more in conflict prevention if Africa is to have a chance of development and prosperity.

The best way to do that is to strengthen mechanisms that can manage tensions before they get violent. The most obvious mechanism for doing this is a strong and effective state, which has systems to resolve disputes between individuals, or groups, before they deteriorate into violence. Africa has had a double problem here. It has many sources of high tension. And its mechanisms for managing them have been weak.

The causes of those sources of tension in Africa vary considerably from one place to another. But there are certain common conditions. Weak institutions and poor governance are risk factors, as are authoritarian rule, poverty and inequality, and the exclusion of minorities from power. States with high levels of corruption and low levels of accountability seem particularly prone to violence. So do economies which are dependent on one or two primary commodities for most of their income. There is a strong link between oil and other mineral wealth and the risk of conflict. Tension over access to land, water and other less lucrative but vital resources is also a factor. And, of course, group identities – such as tribalism, ethnicity or religion – often come into play in the competition for power.

To all this is added the vast quantity of weaponry which is now readily available right across Africa. In some countries an AK-47 Kalashnikov assault rifle can be bought for as little as US$6. Weapons are not a cause of violence, but they are a stimulant of it. When tension turns to violence, it is the proliferation of small arms which makes disputes much more lethal. When AK-47s rather than spears and arrows become the instruments of war the death toll inevitably rockets.

What sparks the tinderbox may be hard to prevent. Triggers can include: controversial elections, coups and assassinations, a sudden influx of refugees from a neighbouring country, and sudden shifts in the economy. Factors like these can convert structural 'proneness' into actual violence. But the solution is not to address these symptoms but rather the underlying causes. Many of this Commission's recommendations in other areas will assist with this.

Investing in development is investing in peace. And this Commission's recommendations as a whole have a fundamental contribution to make to peace. But there are a number of other specific areas which can make a difference:

Ensuring aid does not make matters worse: Aid can do much to reduce the background factors that cause tension and feed conflict. But aid can also inadvertently contribute towards increasing the risk of violence. This is because much aid is short-term and focused on crises. So it often fails to tackle the inequalities and exclusion which are part of the structural causes of conflict. And it routinely underestimates the importance of reform in the policing and justice sector – which is crucial after the fighting stops. Donors should do more to monitor the risk of conflict and modify their development strategies accordingly.

Control of small arms: Many of the largest manufacturers, exporters and brokers of arms to Africa are to be found in G8 and EU countries. The international community has signed a number of control agreements on small arms but these contain gaps which are being exploited by many countries, companies and arms brokers. Measures to control the flow of arms to Africa need to be rigorously enforced. As a matter of priority the international community should begin negotiations on an international Arms Trade Treaty. It must also adopt more effective and legally binding agreements on arms brokering, with common standards on monitoring and enforcement. And donors should support African programmes to tackle the huge amount of weapons already in circulation. A registration scheme for transportation agents, an international aircraft inspection agency and tighter monitoring of the rules on aircraft insurance would also help stop the illegal transportation of arms to Africa and inside it.

Conflict resources: Oil, diamonds, timber and other high-value commodities all fuel Africa's conflicts. Governments use money from their sale to fund increased military activity, at home and abroad. Rebel groups loot oil fields or mines, or extort cash from the firms who operate them. Both sides even sell resources which are still in the ground – pledging advance rights, known as 'booty futures', as the security for loans to buy more arms. All this makes wars last longer and more difficult to resolve.

African governments should be pressed to set up transparent systems that show how they spend the money from mineral wealth. But it should also be made more difficult for warring parties to trade in these 'conflict resources'. Attempts have been made to do this, with some success, through the Kimberley Process – an initiative in which governments, industry and lobby groups joined together to stem the flow of 'conflict diamonds'. The scheme now covers around 98 per cent of the world diamond trade. But each time a new 'conflict resource' needs to be controlled, there is a long process of negotiation. A common definition of conflict resources – and an agreed international framework for acting to control the flow of such goods – would speed up the ability of the international community to react. The UN should set up a permanent body to monitor the trade in conflict resources, and to ensure that sanctions on these resources are enforced.

The role of foreign companies in conflict zones: Better behaviour by foreign companies could improve Africa's climate of peace and security. Sometimes, unwittingly, they make matters worse by hiring security firms to protect their operations. These private armies can become involved in human rights violations. Their arms can be seized by rebel groups. They can crank up tensions further by hiring staff from one social or ethnic group at the expense of another.

But some companies knowingly fuel conflict. They pay substantial sums to oppressive governments or to warlords. Some firms even assist with arms purchases. Some of these actions, like bribery of a local official, are straightforward crimes. Others, like forcibly moving indigenous people from their lands, are illegal under international law. But many of their actions are not crimes – and at present the various voluntary corporate codes of conduct, such as the OECD Guidelines on Multinational Companies, do not provide clear enough guidance on what companies should do in these situations. Such guidelines must be redrafted to include specific provisions on how to avoid creating or exacerbating conflict. The new permanent body in the UN, mentioned above, should be charged with monitoring implementation of these guidelines, with clear disincentives for non-compliance.

Building the capacity to prevent and resolve conflict

Conflict is usually best addressed by those closest to it. Local or national bodies and systems are the first line of defence here. When these fail then regional and international organisations have a role in preventing and resolving violent conflict, and protecting the lives of civilians. Africa's regional economic communities and the African Union have been playing an increasingly active role in this in recent years. These organisations are developing their capacity to detect and mediate conflicts, and conduct peacekeeping when required. The international community has previously made commitments to strengthen African peacekeeping capacity. These pledges should be honoured through, for example, support in training and logistics for the African Standby Force, a continental peacekeeping force being created under the African Union. More than that, the international community must increase investment in more effective prevention and non-military means to resolve conflict.

Developed nations should support Africa's continental and regional organisations in building early warning, mediation and peacekeeping systems. The international community should also assist them with the resources to conduct specific operations – such as mediation, fact-finding missions, and peacekeeping. Unearmarked, regular funding contributions – through, for example, paying for half of the African Union's Peace Fund on a yearly basis – would allow such organisations to have ready access to the resources when they are needed. The work of local organisations such as faith groups should be drawn on by the African Union and African regional organisations to help detect and mediate conflict.

The United Nations has an important role to play in supporting the efforts of these regional bodies – and through its own capacity to prevent and resolve violent conflict. The international community should support the creation of the UN Peacebuilding Commission, as was recently recommended by the United Nations High-Level Panel on Threats, Challenges and Change. This body would engage in both prevention and in planning and co-ordinating post-conflict peacebuilding. The UN defines peacebuilding as encompassing everything from conflict-prevention to rebuilding the institutions and infrastructures of war-torn nations –

and both require tackling causes of conflict such as economic inequality, social injustice and political oppression.

Member states should also support reforms to the management and resourcing of UN peacekeeping operations to speed up troop deployment. They should do more to train their troops for peace operations – including through placing Africa high on the priorities of the 'battlegroups' being formed by the European Union to respond where African nations request military support.

After the fighting stops

When a war ends, peace does not automatically arrive. After disarmament and demobilisation all too often new problems arise – such as how to reintegrate returning soldiers and refugees, who find their homes have been occupied by people who do not welcome them back. And old problems resurface, such as the inequities and resentments which led to conflict in the first place. All that is on top of destroyed infra-structure, a lack of functioning institutions and extreme poverty. Which explains why half of all countries emerging from conflict relapse back into violence within five years.

Post-conflict peacebuilding is a complex task involv-ing many competing demands. The classic approach has been to insist that peace must come first, with economic development thereafter. But what works best to bring a lasting peace is somewhat different.

Obviously security must first be restored. But combatants do not just need to be disarmed, they need to be given jobs and given a stake in the peace. So do returning refugees. War economies need to be dismantled – and alternative economic opportunities created. Steps should be taken to foil those, like warlords, who have a vested interest in wrecking any peace process. The specific requirements of women must be considered, since rape and sexual violence – so widespread during war – have a long-term impact. Special arrangements will be needed for child soldiers. All these processes are long-term and extremely complex which means the frequent delay between peacekeeping operations and the start of social and economic development must be avoided.

Reconciliation is as important as reconstruction in repairing the impact of war on society. This takes a number of forms. Most obviously it is about addressing abuses and human rights violations so that victims begin to feel a sense of justice. Thus, greater aid to the local justice sector is essential. Rebuilding must avoid re-creating those elements of the pre-war order which may have been amongst the causes of the conflict. Peace processes are very political in nature and require sustained support to mediation even after a peace agreement has been made.

Successful post-conflict peacebuilding depends in particular on two things – co-ordination and planning, and financing. Co-ordination and planning would be much enhanced by the creation of the UN Peacebuilding Commission. And post-conflict countries need financing that allows them to begin reconstruction and development efforts early and such aid needs to continue for as much as 10 years after the fighting has ended.

This is a complex and ambitious set of proposals. But then the processes which feed violent conflict are long-term, extremely complex and not amenable to 'quick fix' solutions. If together we can begin to address these issues the future for Africa's children might look very different indeed.

Chapter 6: Leaving no one out: investing in people

Our concern as a Commission has been overwhelmingly for the poorest people of Africa. In Ethiopia the most destitute families are known as 'those who cook water'. In Ghana they are called 'those with two bags' – one for begging in the hungry season, and another for begging in the season of plenty.

Around a sixth of the entire population of sub-Saharan Africa – that is more than 100 million men, women and children – are chronically poor. They are people who experience such persistent poverty that they cannot break free of it using their own resources. They are reliant on day labouring. They have little education and few assets. A period of illness can mean selling the last of what they own to eat. The smallest crisis can tip them over the edge of bare survival into starvation and destitution.

They are individuals and families trapped in vicious circles of poverty. They often choose to grow the least productive crops because those are the ones which have least risk of failure when poor rains come. They dare not risk ambition. And their vicious circles of poverty so easily turn into downward spirals. When parents are unable to invest in the health, education, skills or nutrition of their children, these children will be disadvantaged and more likely to be poor themselves. Another African expression encapsulates these reinforcing cycles of penury; in Zimbabwe they speak of 'poverty that lays eggs'.

But poverty is often about more than a lack of material things. The very poorest people are those who are excluded from the sources of help made available by governments, aid agencies or even the informal support systems of their local community.

All too often the reason is discrimination. Some people are excluded because of their identity – as a woman, as a disabled person, or as a member of a different tribe or ethnic group. Some are discriminated against because of language or the stigma of an illness such as AIDS. Others because they are young people, orphans, albinos, older people, refugees, indigenous peoples or nomads. All lack the power to combat their exclusion.

Two of these groups, of course, are not minorities – women and young people. Women may be Africa's primary carers and providers but they are routinely excluded from information, services and decision-making bodies. Young people – under the age of 17 – are now estimated to make up more than 50 per cent of the continent's population, but have no voice in most decisions which affect them.

The position of women is of particular concern, not merely as a matter of human rights, but also because all the evidence agrees that they make a greater contribution to economic life than do their menfolk. Women are the backbone of Africa's rural economy, accounting for 70 per cent of food production, most of the selling of the family produce and half of the animal husbandry in addition to food preparation, gathering firewood, fetching water, childcare and the care of the sick and the elderly. Women spend most of the earnings they control on household needs, particularly for the children, whilst men spend a significantly higher amount on themselves.

Yet women have fewer opportunities to generate income; they are less likely to attend school; they are subject to harassment and violence; and on widowhood lose their assets. A study in Namibia showed 44 per cent of widows lost cattle, 28 per cent lost livestock and 41 per cent lost farm equipment in disputes with their in-laws after the death of their husband. In many African countries, they lose all rights to cultivate their husband's land.

Africa's challenges will not be effectively addressed unless the exclusion faced by women is tackled across the board. Women must be included and the full power of their development skills unleashed. Women are a key part of the solution to Africa's problems. The same is true of other excluded groups – partly because inclusion is what lessens the tensions which lead to conflict, but mainly because all the evidence is that development works better when no one is left out.

Education for All

Education for All is the title of one of the most exciting pledges that the international community has ever made. At the World Education Forum at Dakar, Senegal, in 2000, the assembled nations committed themselves to providing free primary education for every child in the world by 2015. Adult illiteracy was to be halved and girls given equal treatment across primary and secondary education by 2005. In 2002, a 'Fast Track Initiative' was launched to provide the resources needed to fulfil this promise.

Some progress has been made. Overall numbers of children in primary school in Africa increased by 48 per cent between 1990 and 2001. But provision is patchy. Rural areas are still lagging behind. Girls, disabled children and orphans are still marginalised. Some 40 million children are still not in school. For despite the bold rhetoric of Education for All, the international community is not coming up with the money to match its promises. Donors need now to deliver an estimated US$7-8 billion a year extra to fulfil what they have pledged and to ensure that the whole sector is properly funded – from primary education to secondary and higher, including adult learning and vocational training. This would allow primary school fees to be abolished throughout Africa.

This new money should be spent in three priority areas:

More teachers in the classrooms: Africa is undergoing a teacher shortage of critical proportions. Lesotho has only a fifth of the teachers it needs, and Ghana would need four times more if all children were to be enrolled at primary level. The result of teacher shortages is not just bigger classes but also falling quality of education. Large sums must be invested in teacher training, staff retention and professional development. Donor countries and international financial institutions must change their policies to allow recurrent expenditure – including teachers' salaries – to be paid for from aid.

More girls in the classrooms: Getting girls into school, studies show, is crucial for development. Economic productivity is raised by educating girls. Infant and maternal mortality is lowered. Nutrition and health improve. The spread of HIV is reduced. Providing girls with one extra year of education boosts their eventual wages by 10–20 per cent. And a strong investment is made in the education of the next generation. The removal of school fees would particularly help girls, as would free school meals and school attendance grants. Removing school fees in Uganda almost doubled the number of very poor girls in education. Donors must support this until countries can afford to pay for this themselves, and African governments need to plan more systematically for measures that will achieve greater equality for girls.

Teaching the right things: Across Africa the curriculum must be made more relevant. The existing syllabus is largely limited to academic subjects. Little weight tends to be given to acquiring skills appropriate to developing entrepreneurial attitudes or finding a job. Life skills that address HIV and AIDS are vital. Curriculum development should be led by each African country, drawing on the work of education institutions in the African regions.

Reviving Africa's health services

One in six children in Africa dies before reaching their fifth birthday. This is largely because healthcare delivery systems are at the point of collapse following years of debilitating under-investment. Average spending on health per person in Africa in 2001 was between US$13 and US$21; in the developed world it is more than US$2,000 per person per year. Yet there are glimmers of hope. After the Abuja Declaration in 2000 some 45 per cent of African countries increased their health budgets, with some making impressive increases to reach over 10 per cent of government spending. Donors should support this with an additional US$10 billion a year by 2010, rising to US$20 billion a year by 2015 as health systems are strengthened. Without action here, most other investments in health are doomed to failure. Significant progress can be made in the short term by donors backing the plans to strengthen the foundations of health systems which have been set out by the African Union's NEPAD programme. The following areas must be prioritised:

The health worker crisis: Training and retaining doctors, nurses and other health service personnel has been neglected. Numbers are down, but so is the quality of work. Many of the best have been attracted abroad. Others – frustrated by working without the drugs or equipment they need – have found better paid jobs outside the health service. Radical action is required. Africa's health workforce should be tripled through the training of an additional one million workers over a decade. Salaries should be increased to ensure staff are not wooed from their jobs.

Medicines: Africa needs a predictable supply of medicines and vaccines at a cost it can afford. This means buying drugs in bulk to reduce their price. It means giving large pharmaceutical firms incentives to investigate the diseases that affect Africa, instead of focusing on the diseases of rich countries. Donors should do this immediately by making legally binding commitments to buy these treatments for use in Africa so drug companies are given the incentive to put these new medicines and vaccines into production. Without understanding people's circumstances the right drugs will not be developed. A microbicide gel that would protect women from HIV infection, without men even knowing it is there, is not getting the priority it deserves. Likewise paediatric anti-retroviral treatment is still not available for the five million children living with HIV and AIDs in Africa. Donor governments should also directly fund research, led by Africa, to boost the continent's science, engineering and technology capacity.

Making donors work together: International donors can cause problems by focusing on different diseases in an un-systematic way. They insist on using different drugs from one another. They demand different delivery approaches. They fail to live up to their funding pledges. And they provide funds over short timeframes, which deters African govern-ments from making long-term commitments to projects they know they could not afford to continue if funding dried up after one or two years. Where aid is ineffective donors are sometimes to blame as much as recipients. Donor countries must change their approach. They should all work to a single agreement, to be drawn up by the government in each African country. They should pay for what they have promised. And they should pledge aid over a longer time-frame to allow African governments to plan better. Hospital fees paid by poor Africans bring in, on average, only five per cent of healthcare budgets. For this to be paid by rich nations would cost comparatively little. The abolition of primary healthcare fees in Tanzania would cost only US$31 million. Removing patients' fees in Uganda more than doubled clinic use, with the poorest people increasing their use most. Rich nations should support the removal of fees for basic healthcare, until African governments can afford to take on these costs themselves. Basic healthcare should be free for poor people.

Eliminating preventable diseases: Africa is afflicted by a number of diseases which are entirely preventable. Two-thirds of all the African children who die under the age of five could be saved by low-cost treatments such as vitamin A supplements, oral rehydration salts and insecticide-treated bed-nets to combat malaria. A tenth of all the diseases suffered by African children are caused by intestinal worms that infect 200 million people, and which could be treated for just 25 US cents a child. Many of the 250,000 women who die each year from complications in pregnancy or childbirth (compared to just 1,500 in Europe) could be saved if African governments and donors gave greater emphasis to sexual and reproductive healthcare.

Expanding access to water supply and sanitation

More than 300 million people – some 42 per cent of Africa's population – still do not have access to safe water. Around 60 per cent still do not have access to basic sanitation. Access to clean water would save women and girls the chore of walking an average six kilometres to fetch water, giving them more time for the family, for school and for productive work. Without clean water, anti-retroviral treatment for AIDS sufferers is not as effective and formula milk cannot safely be used to prevent transmission of HIV from mother to child. Better water management can greatly reduce malaria mosquito breeding sites. Yet aid to the sector has fallen by a massive 25 per cent since 1996. This is a short-sighted decline that should be reversed immediately, giving priority to those countries in most need. The G8 already has a comprehensive water action plan for Africa. It is time these commitments are met.

Protecting the vulnerable

Another way of helping poor people is for the state to pay cash allowances for children, widows and orphans, people with disabilities or in old age pensions. This 'social protection' can also be delivered in non-cash benefits like free basic healthcare and education, free school meals, employment-guarantee schemes or skills training for poor people. It can also be delivered by defending people's rights, especially women's and children's right to inheritance and to protection from domestic violence and rape.

African governments are increasing social protection measures because all the evidence shows that is cost-effective – it is much cheaper than the costs of responding after a crisis. Attendance at school has increased to

90 per cent in Zambia since childcare grants of US$6 a month were given to elderly carers of vulnerable children, and nutrition is improving. Including administration this costs US$100 per household a year compared to US$250 a year for food aid. International donors need to back this type of shift in strategy and provide predictable funding for simple benefits on a larger scale. Donors should provide US$2 billion a year, in the first instance, rising to US$5–6 billion a year, for orphans and vulnerable children, including rescued child-soldiers. The money should be paid through families and communities who look after 90 per cent of orphans. With the increasing burden of AIDS these systems will break down without support.

Why AIDS is worse in Africa

The worldwide scourge of AIDS is having a disproportionate impact in Africa where some 62 per cent of the world's 15–24-year-olds who live with HIV are to be found. The scale of the pandemic is chilling. Some 25 million people have died so far, and life expectancy in some southern African countries is now back to pre-1950s levels. A further 25 million Africans are living with HIV, including nearly 40 per cent of the population in Botswana. The human, social and economic implications of all this are not, even now, fully clear.

AIDS does not just devastate a single generation. It attacks three generations – the individual living with HIV or AIDS, but also the children born with the

HIV virus and grandparents who are pressed into levels of childcare and food production for which their advancing years ill-fit them.

It also has an especially destructive impact upon the economy. AIDS primarily affects those of working age who are the productive adults in a population. As many as 90 per cent of people living with HIV and AIDS are aged 15–49. This means that, on present projections, between 20 per cent and 40 per cent of the workforce will be lost in the hardest-hit counties. AIDS hits in the most unlikely ways. Farmers in Zimbabwe who found that their irrigation systems were not working properly discovered that the brass fittings from their water pipes had been stolen for coffin handles.

HIV and AIDS also disproportionately affect women, who often play the most vital role in development. Of the 25 million people living with HIV and AIDS in Africa nearly 57 per cent are women, compared to 47 per cent elsewhere in the world. Data from Zambia indicates that young women are three times more likely to be infected as young men. Women have a greater biological vulnerability to infection but the main risk factors are social: the earlier onset of sexual activity, their lower socio-economic status and their powerlessness to insist on the use of condoms.

The legacy of all this is huge numbers of orphans. Africa had 43 million orphans in 2003. AIDS was responsible for 12 million of those. But that number is set to grow – to 18 million by 2010 and higher for at least another decade. The broader social impacts give cause for concern – in Zambia 71 per cent of child prostitutes are orphans.

The social and economic impact of HIV and AIDS is widespread. Those with a good harvest would once lend to those with a poor one, but in areas with a high incidence of AIDS the amount of surplus for lending has been reduced all round. HIV-affected households save and invest less and their children are more often removed from school. In 20 years' time the economies of developing countries with a high incidence of AIDS will have grown by only a third of what they otherwise could have.

Until recently, HIV and AIDS treatment was a low priority for donors, but funding levels are now rising. It is important however that the international community should not treat AIDS merely as a medical problem. To tackle the disease requires well-functioning health systems and drugs. But it also requires a cultural and social response. In one consultation we heard the tragic story of a woman in Nairobi who explained that it would take her five years to succumb to AIDS, but only months for her baby to die of starvation; thus having unprotected sex for money was the rational thing to do, as it was the only way of keeping her baby alive. Such is the terrible logic of poverty.

AIDS will not be checked until those combating it take on board cultural factors about poverty and choices, traditions and beliefs, perceptions of life and death, witchcraft and ancestral punishment, power hierarchies and gender norms, social taboos and rites of passage, control of female sexuality and the demand for male virility and pressures for widows to marry close relatives of a husband recently dead from AIDS. Health workers must confront such issues, and form partnerships with religious leaders and traditional healers who often have an understanding of culture and of gender and power relationships.

All of this will require additional funding. But the existing commitments, set out in the UN Declaration of Commitment on HIV and AIDS, have not yet been fully delivered. In part this is because donors, again, are not paying what they promised. In part it is because different aid agencies have inconsistent approaches, with some advocating abstinence and others the use of condoms. In part it is because donors are falling over each other in one area, leaving gaps emerging elsewhere. It is essential that rich countries agree a common approach here – with a proper financing plan, agreed roles between agencies and shared principles of good behaviour. But more money is needed too. At present there are insufficient resources to provide a proper range of prevention, treatment and care services. International donors should at once increase their funding to meet immediate needs. Funding should rise by at least US$10 billion a year within five years. Responding to the HIV and AIDS pandemic must be a top priority for the world community.

Getting results

Human development is the area in which the greatest resources will be needed to effect change. Almost half of the extra aid we are recommending should be spent on health, education and HIV and AIDS. But getting results here, as in so many other areas, is not simply about throwing money at the problem. Effective use of these large new resource flows will require comprehensive strategies for delivery and for monitoring results. To this end, African governments must continue to strengthen governance and ensure the participation of ordinary people and local communities in decisions on development. If the international community matches that by delivering on its promises then an enormous amount will be achieved – both in terms of human fulfilment and in building the base for economic growth.

Chapter 7: Going for growth

Thirty years ago Botswana was one of the poorest and most aid-dependent countries in the world. Today the landlocked nation is one of Africa's biggest success stories. It has undergone consistent economic growth to the extent that it is now classified as a 'middle-income' country.

That is not surprising, many people might say. After all, Botswana has diamonds. But Africa so often turns received wisdom upside-down. Look across the continent and it is often precisely those countries with the greatest amounts of mineral and other riches which are in most trouble. In too many countries natural resources bring war. They enrich the elite but for most people they merely increase corruption, poverty, environmental degradation and political instability. Spending on health and education is low in such countries. But Botswana bucks the trend.

Africa is the poorest region in the world. Over the last 30 years its people have, on average, seen virtually no increase in their incomes. The message is clear: without economic growth, Africa cannot make substantial reductions in poverty. Again Botswana is testimony to that. The diamond industry employs only about two per cent of those employees in Botswana's small population who have jobs registered in the formal economy. But proceeds from the diamond industry which have entered the government exchequer have been invested rather than squandered. The economy has grown and the number of people living in extreme poverty has fallen dramatically. (And yet Botswana also highlights a major threat facing Africa's growth and development – it has one of the highest HIV and AIDS rates in Africa).

So Africa is not doomed to slow growth. Botswana is not the only indicator of that. In the last decade, 16 countries in sub-Saharan Africa have seen average growth rates above four per cent, including 10 with rates above five per cent and three with rates above seven per cent. This Commission believes that the recommendations we are setting out should enable African countries to achieve and sustain growth rates of seven per cent by the end of the decade.

What are the common factors to those success stories? Our study of all the available evidence leads us to conclude that, again, governance is at the core. It is the private sector that in the main drives economic growth. But the state has a vital role too – for only it can create the climate within which private entrepreneurial spirit flourishes. Our analysis suggests that there are three essential things the state must do. It must create an economic and political climate which encourages people to invest. It must invest significantly in infrastructure, including in agriculture. And it must have a strategy on how to include poor people in growth by investing in the health and education of its people, tackling the roots of youth unemployment and under-employment and by encouraging small businesses, the most important of which in Africa are family farms.

A safe place to invest

If people are to feel safe about investing their money in a country they need to feel confident about a whole range of things – that the law will be upheld, that contracts will be enforced, that business regulations will not be imposed merely to secure an endless stream of bribes for corrupt officials. They also need stable economic policies, good public financial management systems, predictable and transparent taxation and effective competition laws. These requirements are the same for domestic and foreign investors and in Africa, as in many other developing countries, 80 per cent of investment is domestic and 20 per cent is foreign. These measures work. In Tanzania, an improvement in the investment climate is behind the country's fastest growth in 15 years. In Mozambique, investment climate improvements have resulted in a doubling of private investment.

To spread these improvements across the continent the African Union's NEPAD programme has proposed setting up an Investment Climate Facility. Supporting this idea will not cost much – a total of US$550 million from donors and the private sector over seven years – but the returns on that investment will be significant. The fund will act on key obstacles to doing business, including those identified by the African Peer Review Mechanism and other processes. It will help generate and shape policies across a broad range of areas and give the private sector a voice in deciding priorities on new infrastructure.

One of the most significant barriers to investment for Africa is that outsiders tend to perceive Africa as one large risky country – a view driven by the media and a lack of real information. But we are convinced, from the progress that we have seen across the region in recent years, and from what major international businesses have told us, that this view is wrong and outdated. Those who know Africa are more confident about investing. So the facility should address perceptions too. In addition, developed countries should support a fund of the world's public agency for risk-bearing, the Multilateral Investment Guarantee Agency, to insure foreign and domestic investors in post-conflict countries in Africa. It would also be useful to extend support to domestic investors across sub-Saharan Africa which should boost investment significantly.

Improving infrastructure

Problems with roads, rail, ports, air transport, energy, telecommunications and other infrastructure are cited by the business community and African Finance Ministers alike as one of the chief constraints on economic growth in Africa. And irrigation, energy, water supply and sanitation are among the top priorities for poor people. Africa needs to spend an additional US$20 billion a year on infrastructure investments and maintenance between now and 2015 to sustain a growth rate of seven per cent.

As a first stage developed countries should provide an extra US$10 billion a year to improve Africa's infrastructure. And subject to review, this should be increased again to US$20 billion after 2010. It should avoid funding prestige projects that have so often turned into white elephants in the past but it should cover a whole range of infrastructure projects – from rural roads and irrigation of small plots to larger projects for electric power, ports and regional infrastructure. It should cover maintenance costs for existing infrastructure. Major projects could be built and delivered in partnership with the private sector. Decisions are required now if – given the time-lags which attach to infrastructure investments – these levels are to be reached by the end of this decade.

Down on the farm

Agriculture remains a central part of the economy in every country in Africa. More growth in agriculture is critical to more growth in the wider economy. It is also vital in another way. Since 80 per cent of people depend on farming for their incomes, growth here will have a particular impact on reducing poverty. And since women play the major role in African agriculture it will help combat the inequality women face in African life, which is a strong force for the deepening of poverty.

Agriculture is key to Africa. Evidence from across

the world has shown that industrialisation follows a period of agricultural growth. But farming can itself provide real long-term growth, as rapidly expanding diversification into cut flowers and other non-traditional crops is showing in Kenya, Uganda, and Ethiopia. Yet at present agriculture has just two focuses: growing crops for subsistence and for export to the industrialised world. If a third is added – to grow staple foodstuffs for those parts of Africa which have regular food shortages – then agriculture could bring growth to areas which could be breadbaskets. That would simultaneously redress the situation where at least 25 per cent of the population is undernourished and close to half of African countries experience routine food crises. It would also reduce the need for food imports on the present scale – US\$22 billion worth of food with a food aid complement worth US\$1.7 billion in 2002. With an increasing population, markets in staple foods will be the fastest growing of all agricultural markets in Africa over the next 20 years. Given the current structure of spending, local demand for food will out-pace growth of export markets.

What Africa's agricultural success stories show is that there is no single 'key' to unlock agricultural growth. As with so much in Africa, interventions have to take place simultaneously in a number of areas. Increasing production will be unrewarding without improving markets to sell produce or infrastructure to transport it. A number of interlocking areas must be addressed here, and not one at a time, but together.

Irrigation: Land which is irrigated is much more productive than land which relies on rain-fed agriculture. The crops it can produce are more valuable and yield is less volatile. They are available all year round and are far less susceptible to variability in weather conditions. And irrigation can be increased, with proper consultation processes, without disadvantaging other users of water. The international community should increase funding for irrigation, in support of doubling the area of land under irrigation by 2015, initially focusing on funding a 50 per cent increase by 2010, with an emphasis on small-scale irrigation.

Getting crops to market: As much as 50 per cent of the harvest is lost in many parts of Africa because farmers are unable to get their goods to market. This is double the average in other developing countries. Developed countries should fund the creation of storage facilities, roads and energy infrastructure in Africa's rural areas. An investment of just US$30–US$50 million over a 10-year period could save US$480 million each year for maize alone.

Research and innovation: More research is essential. But it must closely address the problems and needs of local farmers in each place. Many valuable approaches and products, such as hybrid crops, are available already but more work is necessary. In this Africa must choose its own research priorities. The international community should support Africa's efforts to increase innovation in agriculture over the next 10 years. The support should be channelled through African research organisations and universities.

Selling within Africa: Crops for export are currently targeted at the international market. This brings an indispensable annual income of US$17 billion. Yet Africa's internal market could be worth US$50 billion a year. The development of local and regional markets would give smallholders and other producers greater opportunities to sell their food, and also the chance to diversify into new crops. This would require much better internal transport and local financial institutions to provide credit to poor smallholders and poor people.

Land rights and secure tenure: Giving poor people security of tenure on their land in both rural and urban areas is also essential to encourage local investment. Land reform is an intensely political issue in Africa and many donor countries have pulled back from addressing it in recent decades. But African governments must take measures to give poor people, particularly women, access to land and secure rights to their land. When people have title to their land they feel more confident about investing and also can use the title deeds as security to obtain loans.

The challenge of urbanisation

Any strategy for growth and poverty reduction must take seriously the issue of urbanisation. Africa is the fastest urbanising continent in the world – around twice as fast as Latin America and Asia. In 25 years half the entire population will live in cities. Africa is well on the way to European levels of urbanisation – but without the economic base to sustain it. The cities are unable to cope, for this is 'premature urbanisation'. There are no industries to provide jobs and many people – around 72 per cent of the total urban population of Africa live in slums. Constantly threatened by eviction, the living conditions are made worse for such households by the lack of access to water, sanitation and other services. Nearly all of the urban populations in Chad and Ethiopia live in slums. Cities like Nairobi – where almost a million people live in Kibera, the largest contiguous area of slum settlements – are socially unsustainable.

All over the world, the management of cities is the direct responsibility of local authorities. But local authorities are seriously hampered by weak governance and a lack of capacity and resources. City authorities do not have the funds or the necessary professional staff to manage the rapid urbanisation process which has led to a shortfall of millions of housing units. African leaders made this a priority area at the African Union Summit held in Maputo in 2003. Countries like Nigeria, Burkina Faso, Uganda and South Africa have launched national Campaigns on Urban Governance. The growing consensus, under the African Union's NEPAD City Programme, is that strong local governance, decentralisation and systems of community participation are now essential. The international community should empower African governments in planning for rapid urbanisation. Capacity-building is essential at local government level to encourage emerging innovations such as UN-HABITAT's Slum Upgrading Facility, which will set up loan guarantee systems for investment in housing for the urban poor.

The environment and climate change

There is one final factor which will obviously be a
major influence on Africa's future economic growth. It
is the environment. Africa's poor people consistently
highlight the importance of the environment to their
livelihoods. Yet poverty interacts in a two-way process
with environmental problems like desertification, de-
forestation, biodiversity loss, land degradation and the
depletion of fresh water. Improved environmental
management is crucial to overcoming these challenges.
African governments must include considerations of
environmental sustainability in their poverty reduction
strategies. And donors should strengthen environmental considerations in all their work in Africa, in support
of the Environment Initiative of the African Union's
NEPAD programme.

Climate change is a particular worry. The weather
is becoming increasingly volatile in Africa. Rains seem
to be failing more frequently. That is one reason why
we have emphasised irrigation so strongly. Current
predictions suggest a future warming across Africa
of 0.2–0.5°C per decade. Africa is likely to get drier
in northern and southern latitudes and wetter in the
tropics, with significant variation within regions and
countries. Climate variability and the frequency and
intensity of severe weather events are likely to increase.
Rising sea-levels, coastal erosion, saltwater intrusion
and flooding will all impact on coastal communities
and economies. In Tanzania, a sea-level rise of 0.5
metres would inundate over 2,000 square kilometres of

land. Climate-induced threats to agricultural productivity, to food security, water and energy security and to health will all undermine Africa's ability to develop.

The cost of inaction is high. The cost of environmental degradation in Ghana is estimated to be two per cent of national income. In 2000, devastating floods in Mozambique cost 700 lives and left half a million people homeless – and also caused economic growth to fall from eight per cent to two per cent that year. The frequency of these events can only increase with the growing impact of climate change which could be seriously destabilising politically for Africa. Without slowing global warming considerably, it is clear that the livelihoods of millions of Africans will be undermined. Developed countries should therefore set targets for greater use of new cleaner energy technologies to help mitigate greenhouse gas emissions. Donors should give in the region of US$100m, over the next 10 years, to improve climate observation, through the Global Climate Observing System, and build capacity in African research institutions. Donors should also make climate variability and climate change risk factors an integral part of their project planning and assessment, by 2008, and meet their commitments on funding to help African countries adapt to the risks of climate change.

Involving poor people in growth

In all this, growth alone is not enough. Where incomes are unequal most of the benefits from growth go to the wealthy. Growth will not reduce poverty unless poor people are able to participate in it. And policies for growth must actively include, and take care not to exclude, the poorest people in opportunities for health, education and work. Specific action can be taken in the following areas.

The primary source of jobs in Africa is small enterprises, the most important example of which is the family farm. Many of these enterprises operate informally. In Africa, the informal economy covers most agricultural activities and the greater part of urban commercial activities, transport, services, crafts and even small manufacturing industries. The subsistence farmer, the street trader, the taxi-driver, the shoeshine boy – the vast majority of people – all remain excluded from information, business services and access to credit. This is another aspect of the marginalisation of women, for African women often play a pivotal role in informal businesses; in Benin, women traders represent over 90 per cent of total informal trade employment.

Most small businesses – many of them involving a single individual – often rely on family and social networks to raise working capital to start up and grow. In the last decade the growth of micro-finance institutions (MFIs) – so called because they deal in amounts too small to be of interest to commercial banks – has helped to mobilise savings and provide short-term credit to an increasing number of poor people. These MFIs have largely been started by charities, aid agencies and other non-governmental organisations. To magnify the success of MFIs requires banks to become involved, since they have potentially much greater resources, but at present most banks adopt a risk-averse short-term attitude to these smallest of businesses and shy away from them because the potential profit margin is too small.

Foreign businesses can also be of help in fostering opportunity. Multinational companies and major supermarkets in rich countries should go beyond seeing corporate social responsibility as a form of philanthropy and examine the impact their core business activity has on poor people. As a start, businesses must sign up to leading codes of good social and environmental conduct, including on transparency and corruption. But this must go beyond rhetoric or box-ticking. They must make sure their systems are adapted to the needs of African suppliers – including paying them promptly.

Larger foreign and domestic companies can nurture African business skills by targeting local staff for key managerial positions, mentoring the managers of small enterprises, providing access to business training, helping with access to finance. Donor governments should fund initiatives to broker such partnerships.

To assist all this developed countries should set up a US$100 million Africa Enterprise Challenge Fund to increase the access small enterprises have to finance and their ability to make links with other businesses. The new fund should place particular emphasis on tackling youth unemployment and addressing the economic obstacles faced by women. To complement this, developed countries should give US$20 million to the UN's Growing Sustainable Business Initiative in Africa to help foreign and domestic companies to develop commercially viable investment projects to benefit poor people.

These measures on growth and poverty reduction, like all the others we have outlined, are an integral package which combines growth and governance. The mistake of the past has been to think that the one might work without the other.

Chapter 8: More trade and fairer trade

Trade has been a key driver of economic growth over the last 50 years, first in the Western world and Japan, and then more recently in China and India. Developing countries, particularly in Asia, have used trade to break into new markets and change the face of their economies; two decades ago 70 per cent of their trade was in raw materials, but today 80 per cent is in manufactured goods.

Alas, not in Africa. The last three decades, by contrast, have seen stagnation in African countries and a collapse in their share of world trade, which fell from around six per cent in 1980 to two per cent in 2002. This has been caused, in part, by the fact that the composition of Africa's exports has remained essentially unchanged. As more dynamic and competitive regions have made major shifts into manufacturing, Africa has been left behind. The task of catching up gets harder every day.

Analysing this tells us something very interesting. Many people think that Africa's problems in trade come primarily from the trade barriers imposed by rich nations. It is true that those barriers are absolutely unacceptable. They are politically antiquated, economically illiterate, environmentally destructive and ethically indefensible. As we shall say in a moment, they must be scrapped. But – contrary to what is often supposed – there is also another cause, and that is this: Africa simply does not produce enough goods to trade, at least not of the right kind or quality, or at the right price. Addressing those questions, as well as the trade barriers Africa face, are key if Africa is to prosper.

To grow, trade must have the same climate as does the rest of the economy. But there are three other areas in which Africa, with support from the rich world, must make changes: improving transport infrastructure, reducing Africa's internal barriers to trade, and diversifying African economies away from current levels of dependency on primary commodities.

Improving transport infrastructure

Africa needs a functioning transport and communications system to get its goods to market. This is one key area in which rich nations can help. At present the costs and difficulty of moving goods in Africa can be far higher than in richer countries – in many cases double. For landlocked countries transport costs can be three-quarters of the value of exports; transport costs impose the equivalent of an 80 per cent tax on clothing exports from Uganda. These kinds of costs make it extremely difficult to get goods to market at a competitive price. And the problem is not just with land transport. It costs about the same to clear a 20-foot container through the port of Dakar as it does to ship the same container from Dakar to a north European port. This is why transport is such an important element in the infrastructure package we have already recommended above.

Clearing away the roadblocks

Africa has many internal barriers to trade, which damage its ability to grow its way out of poverty. These include excessive bureaucracy, cumbersome customs procedures, and corruption by public servants using bribes to supplement their meagre wages. The African roadblock stands as symbol of many of these. Checkpoints, official and unofficial, are characteristically found on any major African road. The journey from Lagos to Abidjan encounters one every 14 kilometres. In Côte d'Ivoire, to get a single lorry from one side of the country to the other typically adds US$400 to the journey in official payments and bribes.

Customs urgently need reform. Africa suffers from the highest average customs delays in the world, 12 days on average. Estonia and Lithuania require one day for customs clearance; Ethiopia averages 30 days. Customs procedures are often Byzantine in their complexity. Average processing involves 20–30 parties, 40 documents, 200 bits of information, of which 30 have to be repeated at least 30 times. Customs delays throughout Africa add over 10 per cent to the cost of exports. That alone is more damaging than many rich country trade barriers.

Another problem area is the lack of trade between African nations. A mere 12 per cent of all African goods go to other African countries. To improve that requires Africa to reduce its internal trade barriers. That means reducing and simplifying African tariff systems, and eventually creating regional free-trade areas. It means reducing regulatory and other barriers at borders. The size of truck axles and axle load regulations vary between Botswana, Namibia and Zambia. And there are three different rail gauges in Africa.

Many African governments fear that removing these barriers will cut their income. Customs revenues provide up to a quarter of government revenue in Africa. But experience shows that it is possible to reduce tariffs and still maintain revenue. Lesotho tripled its income when equalisation of VAT rates with South Africa and other arrangements reduced smuggling and simplified revenue collection at the border.

African governments have been pressing for decades for rich countries to remove their trade barriers but they could do far more to reduce their own internal restraints on trade. Yet many of these are relatively easy to remove, and it could be done unilaterally. This ought to be an uncontroversial priority for action in Africa. The clean-up of the Mozambique customs service, and the rapid transformation of the Tanzanian port of Dar es Salaam to world standards of efficiency, show what is possible. In Mozambique, goods are cleared 40 times faster than before reforms took place; and customs revenue in the first two years increased by 38 per cent. African governments should make reforms in this area an extremely high priority.

Donors should fund African governments' moves to remove internal tariffs and regulations barriers. They should support reform of customs and port administration, sharing expertise in areas such as automating customs systems. This will not require very substantial donor assistance, but will have major economic pay-offs.

Reducing primary commodity dependency

The biggest single action that Africa could take to reduce its dependency on raw materials is to help large firms and family farms break into new products and activities. Strong support from G8 and EU countries in infrastructure, as described earlier, is key to building this capacity to trade, but they should also help Africa develop the capacity to process agricultural products and improve the productivity and quality of raw materials. They should fund the development of organisations to help small farmers market their produce. Supermarkets could do more to make it easier for household farmers to become suppliers.

Fairer trade

'First do no harm', is one popular summary of the Hippocratic oath taken by doctors through the ages. The maxim should also be applied to the responsibility that the rich world has towards Africa. The trading relationship between the developed and developing worlds has long been one dominated by a complex web of rules, taxes, tariffs and quotas which massively bias the entire business of international trade in favour of the rich. As well as helping improve Africa's capacity to trade competitively, G8 and EU countries must compete more fairly. There are three key areas where developed countries can do more. They should do a deal at the Doha Round of World Trade Organisation talks that genuinely helps development. They should make their existing 'trade preferences' work better. And they should provide cash to help African countries adjust to new trading opportunities.

Agriculture is the activity from which the vast majority of the poorest Africans make their living; by contrast agriculture is not of great economic importance to most developed countries, accounting for a few per cent of national incomes, or less. Yet the agricultural sectors of many G8 and EU countries are the most heavily subsidised and protected in the economies of the industrialised world. Rich countries spend around US$350 billion a year on agricultural protection and subsidies – which is 16 times their aid to Africa. The European Union is responsible for 35 per cent of this, the United States for 27 per cent and Japan for 22 per cent.

These policies have a harmful effect in both the poor and rich worlds. Taxpayers and consumers pay heavily to support their farmers – though, ironically, it is not small farmers in the EU and US who benefit: they get only four per cent of the subsidy, with more than 70 per cent going to the 25 per cent richest farmers, landowners and agribusiness companies. The result is that the EU subsidises sugar beet at such high levels that it is grown in Europe in places where it is economically irrational and inefficient to do so. And in the US subsidies to just 25,000 US farmers, who are paid twice the world market price for cotton, threaten the livelihoods of more than 10 million people in West Africa who produce the crop for a third of the price.

Reform of the EU Common Agricultural Policy is essential, as is further reform of protection and subsidies to American and Japanese agriculture. There are many other ways for rich countries to exercise their right to support their rural areas, such as direct income support to farmers, and investments in rural development and in the environment. Using farm protection to ruin the livelihoods of millions of poor Africans is morally inexcusable.

Action to rectify these trade imbalances must be taken in the following areas:

Taking out the tariffs

Developing countries face disgraceful barriers in the markets of the developed world. Agriculture is the most important export sector, by far, for the poor people of Africa. Yet, knowing that, Europe puts taxes on agricultural produce which are three to four times higher than its tariffs on manufactured goods, and even higher in products of interest to Africa. It is essential that rich countries stop discriminating against the few goods in which Africa has a comparative advantage. G8 and EU countries should accelerate the process of dismantling their trade barriers to give Africa a chance to expand exports – by progressively reducing all tariffs to zero by 2015. This should be a top priority at the

World Trade Organisation's Doha Round negotiations.

And there are new barriers too, such as health and safety standards, where help is needed. If the EU used international standards on pesticides on bananas, instead of its own, African exports would grow by US$410 million. The G8 and EU should apply a 'development test' when designing and setting standards in order to avoid doing major development damage for minimal gains. Rich countries should fund Africa to meet these new standards.

Scrapping the subsidies

Rich countries must also stop subsidising their own farmers to over-produce, undermining world prices, and then dump their surpluses on African markets. When trade ministers meet in Hong Kong in December this year, G8 and EU countries should bind themselves to end all export subsidies and trade distorting support by 2010. As a down-payment, trade-distorting support to cotton and sugar should be scrapped immediately. By doing this and by cutting tariffs they will cut massive wasteful spending, and provide huge benefits to their own public, and to Africa and other developing countries. These reforms could be win-win for everyone. The money saved could be shifted to rural development and environmental needs in the rich world, and aid could be increased to Africa.

Progress on preferences

Contrary to popular belief, which holds that Africa is completely shut out of the markets in rich countries, the continent has substantial access to developed nations' markets through a range of 'preference' schemes – a system by which high-income countries grant partial access to their markets to developing countries.

But these preferences do not work as effectively as they should. They are often temporary and un-necessarily complex (just trying to meet their demands can cost up to 10 per cent of the value of goods entering the scheme). Some have rules which are applied in a deliberately obstructive manner: 'Rules of Origin', intended to determine that the goods exported from the poorest African countries were genuinely made there, are being taken to ludicrous extremes – to the extent that fish are ruled ineligible if the boat they are caught from is Ghanaian but the master of the vessel is South African. The US system has been more helpful for some countries in textiles. It allows the poorest African countries to import garments even if they are made from cloth manufactured elsewhere; 'origin' status is conferred for assembly alone. This approach has created 40,000 jobs in the Lesotho textiles industry.

G8 and EU countries should, as a first step, extend their schemes to cover all low-income countries in Africa so that poor countries such as Ghana, Côte d'Ivoire and Kenya are not excluded. They should apply Rules of Origin to allow countries to source their inputs competitively from anywhere in the world, and requiring from countries only that they add a minimum of 10 per cent of value in their manufacturing or processing industries.

Making these schemes work better could raise African incomes by up to US$5 billion a year, and increase growth across the continent by as much as one per cent.

Assisting with change

Preferences cannot be a permanent system. Eventually Africa must adjust to open competition with the rest of the world. Making those adjustments is a gradual business which is what negotiations at the World Trade Organisation are about. But those changes involve costs. The rich world must help fund this change and smooth the adjustment. This means: helping poor people benefit from the new opportunities created, and assisting those whose incomes may reduce; supporting governments to meet losses in trade revenue; countering the impact of higher food prices for some importing countries; and assisting countries to adjust to losses as the value of preferences erode when rich country trade barriers come down.

Development at Doha

Finally – but perhaps most importantly – what Africa most needs is an ambitious agreement at the Doha

Round of world trade talks by no later than the end of 2006. That cannot happen unless rich countries agree major reductions in their subsidies of their agriculture. It cannot happen without the rich world's trade barriers coming down. It cannot happen without dropping the idea that poor nations must make reciprocal concessions in return for those of rich countries: this is not a level playing field. Trade liberalisation must not be forced on Africa as a condition of trade or aid negotiations. Individual African countries must be allowed to sequence their trade reforms in line with their poverty reduction and development plans, and not be forced to open up their markets to foreign imports on terms which damage their infant industries. The World Trade Organisation allows 'special treatment' for developing countries, but this must work better to deliver what we have described above. And developed countries must provide the increased aid necessary to help Africa adjust to more open markets.

Any deal at Doha must allow reforms to proceed at a pace agreed by Africa, not forced upon it. The discussion must adopt a more transparent and inclusive style of decision-making than is often the norm at WTO negotiations. And it must ensure that poorly staffed African governments can get a fair deal when involved in highly complex rules-based trade negotiations in which rich countries have large teams of highly paid lawyers.

While Doha is a multilateral process, bilateral measures – such as free trade agreements negotiated between the US or EU, and Africa – can cause harm by forcing additional demands. The EU must ensure that the Economic Partnership Agreements it is currently negotiating with Africa are designed primarily for development, guided by the same principles that we call for in the Doha Round – and providing African products with full access to the EU market, with the EU not demanding concessions from Africa in return, and providing the aid necessary to increase Africa's capacity to trade. Such negotiations must pay adequate attention to the impact on poverty.

All of these policies – increasing opportunities for trade, and lifting restraints on trade – must be pursued together. We realise this is an ambitious agenda but we believe it to be a realistic one. Anything less will not offer Africa the opportunities it needs to increase trade, in both traditional products and new ones. And it should not be separated from the other recommendations of this Commission. Africa will never break out of its interlocking vicious circles with piecemeal solutions and policy incoherence.

Chapter 9: Where will the money come from?

When you are stuck with a really tough problem, Albert Einstein once said, you have to change your mental approach entirely. More of the same will not get you anywhere. You have to move your thinking to a different level.

The same is true when it comes to Africa, and the question of how the world is to finance the changes that are required. The problems we are addressing are huge. They are the result of three decades of stagnation. To agree a few more incremental steps along the road already travelled will get us nowhere. Change requires a quantum leap. That is why we are suggesting a doubling of aid to Africa within the next three to five years.

That is a lot of money. But this is not a time for timidity. Get it right and in two decades we should be looking at a strong and growing Africa, for which aid is needed in ever-decreasing amounts, as has happened in Asia. Get it wrong and many of the children of Africa will be doomed to a life of abject misery as their mothers and fathers have been – and things will actually get worse.

Three changes are necessary now: continued improvements in governance in Africa, a substantial increase in aid from the international community and a significant change in the way donors do business in Africa.

The major programme of reform we have outlined – in governance, public investment and social expenditure – will cost, we estimate, an additional US$75 billion a year. There is no prospect of Africa paying for this alone. At present Africans pay as much or more tax, proportionate to their income, as the citizens of other low-income countries. But it can never be enough to break out of the present deadlock. So how are we to finance the extra investment and expenditures needed?

What we propose is a two-stage approach. First we recommend that African governments and donors, over the next three to five years, get to a halfway point. That will mean a third of the initial amount of resources needed (roughly US$12.5 billion) being provided by Africa – through increased tax revenue coming from extra growth. Two-thirds of the resources (US$25 billion) will come from an increase in aid. Progress should then be reviewed. Subject to improvements in African governments' managerial and administrative capacity, and improvements in the way aid is delivered, we would recommend a further increase in aid of US$25 billion a year. Africa can find its increased contribution by leveraging other sources of financing, including domestic savings, foreign and domestic investments, and by more efficient and transparent public finances.

To attempt to give extra aid faster than that would not be sensible because, as we shall set out shortly, at present Africa does not have the capacity to handle it effectively – though it is important not to overstate the case. This two-stage proposal is both realistic and

practical. Anything less will not give African economies the kick-start they need.

There may be those who ask whether aid is the right
solution at all. Certainly Africa can and should pay
for part of the required increase in expenditure. But
the amounts needed to achieve the critical mass necessary for change are of such an order that the bulk will
have to come from the rich world. Aid is the only
credible source of this. And the US$25 billion that is
required in the first stage is, after all, only an extra 0.1
per cent of the income of rich countries; just 10 cents
in every US$100.

Does aid work?

Extensive studies done in recent years show that, when
a strong commitment is made to change governance,
aid works. It is bringing education – free to 1.6 million
children in Tanzania in 2002. It is bringing healthcare
– increasing the number of poor out-patients by 87 per
cent in Uganda since 2000. It eradicates disease –
smallpox was wiped out by a little more than US$100
million worth of targeted aid. It brings growth –
Mozambique grew at an astonishing 12 per cent in
the 1990s, while aid accounted for about 50 per cent of
national income. All of these examples are repre-
sentative of many more. Analysis by the World Bank
suggests that average rates of return on its aid projects
in Africa exceed 20 per cent.

Yet despite this, the system for allocating aid to
African countries remains haphazard, uncoordinated

and unfocused. Some donors continue to commit errors that, at best, reduce the effectiveness of aid. At worst, they undermine the long-term development prospects of those they are supposed to be helping. Rich countries pursue their own fixations and fads, often ignoring the needs prioritised by African governments. The amounts they give are unpredictable, sometimes varying by as much as 40 per cent from one year to the next. They tie aid so that it can only be used to buy the donor's own products or services – effectively reducing the value of aid by as much as 30 per cent. Tied aid should be scrapped. They continue to attach unnecessarily detailed conditions to aid packages. They insist on demanding, cumbersome, time-consuming accounting and monitoring systems – and refuse to link with the recipient's systems. They are insufficiently flexible when it comes to reallocating aid to new priorities in the face of a national emergency. They don't respond quickly, or appropriately, when natural or economic disasters strike, such as droughts or floods, unexpected hikes in oil prices or falling commodity prices.

It is time to change all that to bring the bad aid up to the standards of the good aid, and to make this change decisively and quickly. G8 and EU governments should do this immediately, in the following key areas:

More aid should be provided as grants rather than loans. This will avoid adding to Africa's existing debt burden. It will also allow aid to be targeted in places where loans are inappropriate – through regional bodies, local government or faith communities.

Aid should be pledged over longer timeframes and be predictable. Up to 80 per cent of African education spending, for example, goes on teachers' salaries. How can governments train and employ more teachers if they do not know whether the funds will still be there to pay their salaries in three, five or ten years' time?

Aid should be aligned to the priorities and systems of African governments, not to those of donors. Where governance is already good, aid should be paid directly into African government national budgets; where not, aid should wherever possible be channelled in ways that improve local systems rather than trying to bypass them.

Rich countries should harmonise their aid policies and delivery systems to reduce the burdens placed on already stretched African governments.

Donors should encourage African governments to respond primarily to the needs of their people, rather than to the strictures and processes of the international community. For aid to be effective it has to be accountable to the people it is meant to benefit.

A US$4 billion a year fund should be established, possibly within the African Development Bank, to cushion African governments from unanticipated shocks to the economy, such as natural disasters and sudden drops in commodity prices caused in part by the unfair global trade regime, which can destabilise the economy and reduce national income by up to three per cent.

How much aid can Africa usefully absorb?

There is one other pivotal issue. Despite the glaring needs across Africa, there is a limit to the number of roads, dams, schools, and clinics that can be built and serviced effectively in any one year. Africa only has so many technical experts and managers to plan, budget and build. There are also other factors – macro-economic, institutional, physical, human, social, cultural and political – which limit the amount of aid Africa can absorb and use effectively in one go. The shorthand which economists use to describe this is 'absorptive capacity'. No analysis of aid can afford to ignore this problem and the Commission has examined it very carefully.

Absorptive capacity depends critically on two things: African governance and the quality of the rich world's aid. Donor countries should, as we have said, both support changes in governance and move strongly to improve the quality of aid. The evidence we have suggests that African governance has already improved, as has the quality of aid, to the extent that US$25 billion extra could be used effectively now. And, if current trends continue and outside support works effectively, five years from now Africa will be able to absorb another increase of a similar order.

Is extra aid forever?

There are those who fear that aid invariably induces dependency. This only happens where economic growth does not occur. When growth comes, aid can fall away. This has happened around the world. For example, South Korea has switched from being a recipient of aid in the 1960s to a contributor of aid in the 1990s.

It has happened in Africa too where, as we have seen, Botswana has been transformed from one of the countries most dependent on aid into a middle-income country no longer in need of significant amounts of external assistance. Donors have begun to phase out their funding there. Botswana has done this through strong political leadership and sound management (including in the aid sector where the government was willing to reject aid which did not fit in with its policies and priorities). The number of people living in extreme poverty has fallen dramatically. With high economic growth, Botswana proves, the need for aid falls slowly away.

What about debt?

What Africa does not need is negative aid – which is what the payments to service its debt, in effect, constitute. Sub-Saharan Africa's total external public debt totalled US$185 billion in 2003. That burden clings like a heavy parasite to the body of every man turning the soil in his field, every woman carrying a heavy pot of water from the well, and every child who cannot go to school. With debt, progress is slowed. Countries with high levels of public debt generally have lower rates of economic growth.

Much of Africa's debt, given the current state of its economies, can never be repaid. The international community has made some acknowledgement of this in the past, with programmes of debt reduction. It is time for the developed world to own up to the fact that where debt could never be repaid, debt 'relief' merely relieves the creditor of a balance sheet fantasy. And it perpetuates the situation whereby debt discourages private investment, and increases the flight of capital out of African countries.

More than that, decisions on debt reduction have been made primarily taking into consideration how 'sustainable' a country's debt was – that is to say how much in debt repayments it could afford while still functioning as an economy. This never bore much relation to reality: indeed, only four countries have succeeded in getting to 'sustainable' levels of debt according to the narrow criteria of the HIPC debt-relief programme. Decisions on debt relief should be taken in accordance with the same poverty-reduction criteria that are used for making decisions on aid – that is, whether it will be well used to promote both the growth and participation in growth by poor people which together reduces poverty.

For poor countries in sub-Saharan Africa which need it, the objective must be 100 per cent debt cancellation as soon as possible. This must be part of a financing package for these countries to achieve the MDGs, as promised in Monterrey and Kananaskis. The key criterion should be that the money be used to deliver development, economic growth and the reduction of poverty for countries actively promoting good governance. Accordingly, work should begin immediately to establish a transparent debt compact to include all sub-Saharan African low-income countries, including those excluded from current schemes. It should cancel debt stock and debt service by up to 100 per cent, and cover multilateral and bilateral debt. As an urgent measure, financing should immediately be put in place to provide 100 per cent multilateral debt service cancellation, where this is necessary to achieve the MDGs.

Finally, relief should end in 2015 to avoid the risk of new loans being taken with the expectation that they subsequently will be written off.

Raising the money

There are a number of ways in which the additional aid could be raised. Several nations have recently committed themselves to reaching the UN target of giving 0.7 per cent of their national income in aid. Other G8 and EU nations should now follow this example and announce timetables for reaching the 0.7 per cent target. Within these aid budgets, particularly in the context of a potential global increase in aid of US$50 billion, there is a strong case for reallocating money so that less goes to middle-income countries and more goes to poor countries, especially Africa, which is the only region in the world that is not growing.

But this will not be enough. To provide the amounts which are essential to give Africa the momentum it needs will require a lot of assistance now. Investing in the education of children, in improving health standards, in building infrastructure, in improving governance and in creating a climate which encourages people to invest in creating new jobs is, of course, good for poor people today. But it also establishes a stronger base for future economic growth. And all of these measures improve the prospects for the success of one another. Done together they can create the opposite of a vicious circle – a virtuous one. But if they are done separately, in piecemeal efforts, spread over time, they will lose that mutually reinforcing effect. That is why it is necessary to take the aid money to be pledged for the next decade and to spend a large amount of it up-front. Not to do that would be to fail to learn the lessons of the past.

This front-loading of aid is not just right in humanitarian terms – because it swiftly attacks today's poverty – it also makes economic sense. Investing more aid now will give higher returns on the overall investment. G8 and EU countries should front-load their aid commitments so that a critical mass of money can be deployed soon. They should commit now to a phased doubling of aid for Africa. This should be financed through the immediate launch of the International Finance Facility (IFF). Under this, donors would make long-term and binding pledges on aid; using these commitments as security the IFF would raise money now from the international capital markets by issuing bonds, which donors' future pledges would repay. The IFF would not require an increase in aid budgets from donor governments; it is founded on the additional aid commitments for the future that many countries have made, in particular the countries with commitments to reach the 0.7 per cent target. Nor would it require a doubling of aid bureaucracies, since it could work more through existing systems to pass more money directly into Africa government budgets.

An additional and complementary approach is to raise finance through international taxes, levies or lotteries. One example would be a voluntary levy on airline tickets to reflect the costs inflicted by carbon emissions. A number of other innovative proposals have been suggested to help address the funding gap. Further work should be undertaken to come up with specific practical proposals.

Doubling aid to Africa may sound ambitious. In reality it amounts to giving every man, woman and child on the continent just an extra 10 US cents a day. If efforts now are too small and uncoordinated to be effective, the world will be faced with the prospect of a permanent aid programme to Africa.

Chapter 10: Making it happen

How then will we ensure that the world delivers on what this Commission has proposed?

First, by ensuring that Africa's development is shaped by Africans. History has shown that development does not work if it is driven from outside. Regardless of how well intentioned outside donors may be, they will never fully understand what Africa requires. 'No matter how long a log stays in the water it doesn't become a crocodile' as one of our Commissioners, President Benjamin Mkapa of Tanzania put it, quoting a proverb from the Bambara people of Mali. Africans must lead, and the rich world must give support.

The history of the past few years should make eliciting that support easier. Africa's changing actions are creating the case for strong external assistance. And conditions for success have not been better for 30 years.

To make good that promise will take a clear programme of action, based on sound evidence. That is what we have sought to provide here. The development community has learned much about what works and what does not, from the successes and failures in Africa in the last few decades. That evidence has been behind the proposals in this report.

We have tried to make our proposals clear and specific. But we have also tried to show that Africa's interconnected problems can be solved only by an interconnected raft of proposals. Piecemeal solutions are doomed to fail. A big push is required on many fronts at once.

If those solutions are to work, changes must come within many institutions, both in Africa and in the developed world. Inside Africa the priority is strengthening institutions by building their capacity and making them more accountable to ordinary people. That will not work without increased financial support from the rich world.

The best way to deliver that support is to put aid into African government budgets and let them prioritise the spending of it. This direct budget support ensures that aid goes most effectively to the government's agreed development priorities. It also keeps the additional monitoring and reporting costs for African governments to a minimum. It should be predictable and long term, though clearly there must be break-clauses if the internal situation changes radically.

But this will only work where a government has a clear development strategy in place – and where the budget system is open and transparent. Where this is not the case a sector-wide approach to a particular area such as education or health may be more appropriate. And where governance is too poor for donors to have confidence in sector-wide approaches aid may best be paid into specific projects run by aid agencies or other non-governmental organisations. Project support of this sort can make a real difference at grassroots level, but by definition cannot help build the capacity within government which is a prerequisite for long-term development – which is why we encourage donors to move wherever possible along the spectrum from project aid to sector-wide approaches, and from these to direct budget support. At the very least, however, donors should ensure that projects do not run counter to African governments' development and budget priorities. Nor should they undermine African efforts to improve the capabilities of government ministries.

Africa's transnational organisations need support too. Its Regional Economic Communities have great potential – as the 'building blocks' of the African Union – but have as yet only weak capacity and are all too often diverted from long-term development issues by crises or conflict. They require the support of the international community, as does the African Union and its NEPAD programme, the Economic Commission for Africa and the African Development Bank whose shareholders should ensure that it now develops the vision and takes the steps to become the pre-eminent financing institution in Africa. It is these organisations which have developed the 'agenda for change' which is Africa's new hope.

Change is necessary too in the institutions of the developed world. Donor counties must co-ordinate their work better with one another, and also with Africa's national strategies to reduce poverty. The World Bank, IMF and World Trade Organisation and the UN all need to do better on Africa.

The World Bank must shift more of its resources, including staff, to Africa, and must provide more of its assistance as grants rather than loans in poor countries. It should focus more staff on states with weak and unstable institutions. It should make longer-term aid commitments and increase the predictability of its aid flows. And it should improve its co-ordination with other donors, including UN agencies, who should strengthen their own co-ordination at country level.

The IMF could help developing countries by assessing and publicising information about their budget and accounts, so enabling citizens to hold their governments accountable as well as supporting external assessments, such as those for debt negotiations. It should avoid creating ill-judged limits on what countries can spend and should promote a better allocation of grants to poor countries. It should change its corporate culture to show greater flexibility.

Both the Bank and the Fund need to micro-manage less and reduce the amount of conditions they place on poor countries. The only conditions that should be laid down are that African government policies must focus on development, growth and poverty reduction, and that in their handling of their budgets they must be transparent and accountable to their voters. If African governments are left to make the hard decisions themselves, as more and more are showing themselves willing to do, reforms are more likely to stick. 'One who bathes willingly with cold water does not feel the cold' says a Tanzanian proverb.

In World Trade Organisation (WTO) negotiations, rich countries should seek only minimal concessions from poor countries in return for making major concessions themselves. The reciprocity traditional in trade negotiations will not help Africa overcome the huge obstacles it faces. Nor should poor countries be blackmailed into accepting a plethora of complex arrangements as the price for admission to the WTO. Declarations to this effect should be made by rich-country ministers at the next WTO meeting.

The World Bank, IMF, and WTO management must prepare strategies for Africa that reflect these points, preferably for their 2005 annual meetings. The WTO strategy should be agreed at the organisation's 2005 ministerial meeting. What is fundamentally important is finding ways of increasing the accountability of these institutions to their shareholders and clients. One option is the creation of a monitoring group to assess the quality of donor assistance in each country; this could be independent or it might be made up of representatives of the recipient government and the donors. But what is crucial is that Africa is given greater say in decision-making in these multilateral bodies. African representation should be increased on the UN Security Council. Africa should be given a stronger voice on the executive boards of the World Bank and IMF. Moreover, the strategic direction of these institutions should be put in the hands of decision-making councils whose members would be accountable to political leaders with authority to speak for the member countries.

Responsibility for these reforms lies with the political leaders of the member countries, who must make these international financial institutions more open and publicly accountable. As a signal of this the top jobs in the IMF and World Bank should no longer be restricted to candidates of Europe and the United States but should be filled through open competition. If reform is not forthcoming the international public will be forced to the conclusion that these institutions, established after the Second World War, are becoming increasingly irrelevant in our post-Cold War, post-apartheid, post-11 September world.

Our proposals add up to a detailed blueprint but they will do little good without mechanisms to monitor them. There are a number of existing bodies which might be charged with the task but they either have limited briefs or no teeth to enforce delivery. Therefore, to add extra force to our recommendations this Commission proposes an independent mechanism to monitor progress on the implementation of what we have proposed. This could, for example, be led by two distinguished and influential figures who carry weight in the international community, one African and one from the donor community, who could produce a short, open and focused annual report. They should be supported by a small unit within an existing international or African institution.

But no matter how clear the recommendations, or diligent the monitoring process, none of this will happen without political will. Only that will close the yawning gulfs of the past between commitments and delivery. To build that political will requires Africa to become an issue which cannot be ignored in the domestic politics of G8 countries.

We know that – with the help of parliamentarians, the media, the aid agencies, the churches and other faith groups, the trades unions, the African Diaspora and the business community – this can be done. Individual voices and grassroots action can make a profound difference. The Jubilee 2000 campaign proved that. It was started by two individuals and ended with a million people on the streets worldwide, demanding that the debt of poor countries be dropped. The governments of the rich world were forced to listen and US$100 billion worth of bilateral debt was written off.

That is why this year's international Global Call For Action (Make Poverty History) campaign is so important. We hope that 2005 will be the year when 100 per cent of the remaining multilateral debt is cancelled. At the launch of that campaign, in London in February, Nelson Mandela told a crowded Trafalgar Square: 'In this new century, millions of people in the world's poorest countries remain imprisoned, enslaved and in chains. They are trapped in the prison of poverty. It is time to set them free.'

Only a sense of public indignation at that state of affairs will bring our politicians to make the commitment to take the necessary decisions to do that. And this time to stay the course.

Broken promises and squandered opportunities

Anyone drawing up a plan for a major programme of action such as the one proposed by this Commission becomes acutely conscious of one thing. The relationship between Africa and the developed world is a story of hopes raised, and constantly dashed – of promises broken and opportunities squandered. African leaders themselves, of course, cannot be acquitted on this charge. Africa has fallen short on its commitments too.

Pledges to commit 15 per cent of national budgets to health have not yet been realised. Sweeping commitments to gender equality have yet to be turned into action. But the catalogue of unfulfilled undertakings by the leaders of the wealthy world is a source of some shame.

Pledges of 'education for all' have gone unfunded. So have commitments on HIV and AIDS. Initiatives to curb corruption are unratified and unimplemented. The world says 'never again' after every major atrocity, but turns a blind eye to the trade in small arms. Codes of conduct by multinational companies remain mere exercises in public relations. Trade rules are applied vexatiously. Promises on aid are seen as impossible targets. Debt forgiveness schemes are hedged about with intractable restrictions. Wealthy nations make well-intentioned pledges at international conferences only to later decide that the promises, or their timetable, were unrealistic. Goals are set, reset, and recalibrated yet again so that all the rich world ends up doing is mitigating the extent to which it has failed. The gap between promises and reality never closes.

Today the world community has before it another great pledge. Five years ago in New York every world leader, every international body, almost every single country, signed up to a historic declaration. The Millennium Declaration reflected a shared commitment to right the greatest wrongs of our time. The Millennium Development Goals were an extraordinary plan which promised that by 2015 every child would be at school. That by 2015 avoidable infant deaths would be prevented. That by 2015 poverty would be halved.

But already those noble ambitions are receding into the distance. Despite the pledge to find the necessary resources – and despite a renewal of the commitment at the UN conference on Financing for Development in Monterrey in 2002 – Africa is well behind target on reaching all the goals. A measure of how far is graphically revealed in the UN Millennium Project report – Investing in Development – which was published in January 2005.

On current projections the halving of poverty will come not by 2015 but by 2150 – that is 135 years late. Africans know that it is often necessary to be patient but 135 years is too long to ask people to wait, when their children are dying while the rest of the world has the medicines to heal them. It is too long to wait for justice.

The Millennium commitment was a bond of trust, perhaps – to quote another of our Commissioners, the UK Chancellor Gordon Brown, 'the greatest bond of trust ever pledged between rich and poor'. Promises made to poor people should be considered particularly binding. The cheque offering international justice must not be returned, to use a vivid phrase of Martin Luther King, with the words 'insufficient funds' scrawled upon it. The danger we face today is that what began as the greatest bond between rich and poor for our times now risks turning into the greatest betrayal of the poor by the rich of all time.

The problem is not that the Millennium Development promise was wrong, the pledge unrealistic or the commitment unnecessary. It is that the world has been too slow in developing the means to honour it.

Fulfilling the commitment requires strong and urgent action. The Commission for Africa's programme of action – improving African governance and infrastructure, giving the continent further substantial debt reduction, doubling aid to halve poverty and opening up trade opportunities – shows that there is a realistic way of doing that. Without a programme like that the Millennium Development Goals will perish as yet another pious aspiration. And Africa will remain, in the words of the chairman of this Commission, a scar upon the conscience of the world.

Why bother?

There will be those who will say we have been too ambitious or unrealistic. Grand overviews have been tried before, they will say. In the late 1970s the Brandt Commission spent seven years analysing the issue of global poverty. Its report, North–South, proposed a number of reforms to the world economic system with the aim of integrating Third World countries into the global economy. The changes which followed were only piecemeal, but this need not always be the fate of such initiatives. People were scornful too after the Second World War when the Marshall Plan was announced. In 1948 the US Secretary of State, General Marshall, faced with a Europe in ruins, proposed a wide-ranging plan for reconstruction. He started with a narrow view of emergency aid but quickly came to the conclusion that there were deep social and economic issues that must be addressed.

The result was that the richest country in the world – the USA – agreed to transfer one per cent of its national income, every year for four years, to finance the development of a ravaged post-war Europe. Rich countries are now much richer and the additional US$25 billion a year we are proposing as a first stage is just an extra 0.1 per cent of their income. It should be used to take action in a broad number of areas, simultaneously, as the Marshall Plan did. The Marshall Plan worked. We should remember that.

What Africa requires is clear. It needs better governance and the building of the capacity of African states to deliver. It needs peace. It needs political and economic stability to create a climate for growth – and a growth in which poor people can participate. It needs investment in infrastructure and in the health and education systems which will produce a healthy and skilled workforce as well as a happy and fulfilled people. It needs to trade more, and on fairer terms than the rich world has allowed to date. It needs more debt-relief. It needs aid of a better quality than at present. And it needs a doubling of aid to pay for this.

Without simultaneous co-ordinated undertakings across a whole range of areas Africa's economic revival will be halting if it happens at all. But if Africa gets the 'big push' we recommend, the continent ought – sooner than many people might expect – be in a better position to stand on its own feet, and eventually make aid a thing of the past.

In all of this Africa must take the lead, but in all of it Africa will require considerable support from the rich world, which will have to give more and also change its behaviour – on international trade, on debt-relief and on including Africa more in the considerations of its institutions.

Why should the rich world bother? For a start, out of self-interest. A stable and growing Africa will provide a market of several hundred million people into which the rest of the world can sell its goods and services. Africa has the potential to be transformed from a place of privation to one of opportunity. It will also provide a stable source of supplies. Africa holds seven per cent of world oil reserves, and generated 11 per cent of global oil exports in 2000. By 2015, West Africa will provide 25 per cent of the oil imports into the United States. And its richness in natural resources is not confined to the more traditional commodities. It is the primary source of coltan, the essential component of the world's mobile phones. As the world changes and grows it is likely that Africa's rich resources will continue to be vital to the world's prosperity.

By contrast, if Africa persists in a state of insecurity and economic stagnation that will not just be bad for Africans, it will be bad for the rest of the world. It will lead to still more powerful pressures for migration, legal or illegal. And an Africa which is unable to control the spread of disease will not only condemn countless numbers of African children, women and men to an unnecessary death, it will also be a source of disease for the world as a whole in an era of globalisation.

Moreover – as the events of September 11th 2001 have emphasised all too starkly – an Africa with failing states and deep resentment can become a source of conflict which is not only internal but spreads across continents in international terrorism and crime. Cells of groups linked to al-Qaeda are thought to be in operation in Kenya, Ethiopia, Somalia and Sudan and terrorist attacks have already taken place in East Africa. Indeed al-Qaeda's first outrages were in Africa, with the bombing of the US embassies in Nairobi and Dar es Salaam. There are also concerns about increasing links between North and West African terrorist groups, for example in Algeria, Morocco and Mali. These groups, hiding in places where they can plot undisturbed by weak governments, threaten security and prosperity within Africa, with many Africans dying in attacks and tourism and other investments being undermined. They are also a threat to the whole world community.

But this Commission believes that there is something much deeper that motivates us. There is something greater, more noble and more demanding than just our shared needs, and linked destinies. Our common interest, the title of our report, is defined by our common humanity.

Different Commissioners have spoken of this in different ways. Our chairman, the British Prime Minister, Tony Blair, has spoken of 'recognising the common bond of humanity'. The activist and musician, Bob Geldof, has talked of a mission 'to extend the hand of sympathy and shared humanity to reach above the impenetrable roar and touch the human beings on the other side'. The Ethiopian Prime Minister Meles Zenawi, has used the word 'solidarity' – a term which means not some feeling of vague compassion but a firm and persevering determination for us all to commit ourselves to the common good because we are all really responsible for all.

There is more to this than the kindness of strangers. It is about a journey from charity to justice or what in Zulu and other Bantu languages is called *ubuntu* which insists that the very identity of each person is bound up with others in a community of all. 'I am what I am because of who we all are', it says. In a globalised world our sense of *ubuntu* must extend right across the planet. The more global the market, the more it must be balanced by a global culture of solidarity, attentive to the needs of the weakest. Interdependence is, in its most profound sense, a moral issue. Our common humanity is violated by the extreme poverty we all see in Africa. And that is what propels us to demand action against deprivation and despair on behalf of other people we may never meet in far-away places.

We are one moral universe. And our shared moral sense makes us recognise our duty to others. We, as a mixed group of African and non-African Commissioners, have in our shared enterprise experienced some sense of this as we have been bound together in the interests of our common good.

The time is ripe for change. That is the conviction of us all. Acting together we have the power to shape history. To do nothing would be intolerable. To do something is not enough. To do everything we can is not only a requirement, it is our clear duty. Now is the time to act.

Recommendations

Africa has begun to make progress in the long battle against poverty. But to sustain that will require a stronger partnership between African nations and those of the rich world. That means action, and change, on both sides.

Africa must take the lead in this partnership, take on responsibility for its problems and take ownership of the solutions – which are far more likely to work if they spring from African insights and judgements than if they are imposed from outside. The international community, for its part, must cease to do those things by which it harms or disadvantages the world's poorest people. It must do what it can to support the reforms which are underway in Africa; these must accelerate significantly if the continent is to prosper and poor people are to share in that prosperity. It must support Africa's regional initiatives, including the African Union and its NEPAD programme, to work together to generate and promote these reforms.

Some of our recommendations – on infrastructure, on health, on education – require significant transfers of money from the developed world to Africa. Others – underpinned by new approaches to African cultures – require changes to behaviour, ways of working and priorities. Others call on the international community to stop doing things which damage Africa. All these should be seen as an integrated package. Partners must work together to implement this package with commitment, perseverance and speed, each focusing on how they can make the most effective contribution.

A: Recommendations on Governance and Capacity-Building

Weak governance has blighted the development of many parts of Africa to date. Weak governance can include bad government policies and an economic and political climate which discourages people from investing. It can also include corruption and bureaucratic systems that are not open to scrutiny and therefore are not answerable to the public. And it includes a lack of accountability and weakness in mechanisms to ensure that people's voices are heard and their rights upheld, such as parliaments, the media and the justice system.

At the core of the governance problem in many parts of Africa is the sheer lack of capacity of national and local government ministries, and the problems of recruiting and keeping skilled staff, equipped and motivated to do their job. The continent's regional and pan-African organisations, including the African Union and its NEPAD programme, which are so important to Africa's future, also need strengthening.

Investing in capacity-building

• Developed countries should give strong support – both political and financial – to Africa's efforts to strengthen pan-African and regional bodies and programmes, including the African Peer Review Mechanism.

- African governments should draw up comprehensive capacity-building strategies. Donors should invest in these, making sure that their efforts are fully aligned with these strategies rather than with their own competing priorities and procedures.
- Skilled professionals are key to building improvements in the administration and technical ability which Africa so gravely lacks. The international community should commit in 2005 to provide US$500 million a year, over 10 years, to revitalise Africa's institutions of higher education and up to US$3 billion over 10 years to develop centres of excellence in science and technology, including African institutes of technology.

Increasing accountability and transparency

- Parliaments in both developed and other developing countries should establish partnerships to strengthen parliaments in Africa, including the pan-African parliament.
- Independent media institutions, public service broadcasters, civil society and the private sector, with support from governments, should form a consortium of partners, in Africa and outside, to provide funds and expertise to create an African media development facility.
- Developed country governments, company shareholders and consumers should put pressure on companies to be more transparent in their activities in developing countries and to adhere to international codes and standards for behaviour.

- The international community should give strong political and financial support to schemes such as the Extractive Industries Transparency Initiative (EITI) to increase the transparency of payments made to, and received by, governments and should encourage its acceptance by all resource-rich African countries. It should support the development of criteria and a means of validating EITI implementation; and support and fund capacity-building among public servants as well as civil society, by contributing to the EITI Multi-donor Trust Fund.
- Principles of transparency such as those in EITI should be extended to other natural resource sectors, including forestry and fisheries.
- Timber importing countries should ensure they do not trade in illegally acquired forest products and should procure only legally sourced timber and products.

Corruption

Corruption is a systemic challenge facing many African leaders. They must demonstrate renewed political will to fight it at all levels in the economy and society. Many African nations have begun this task. Increased transparency by African governments will assist this. But fighting corruption involves tackling those who offer bribes as well as those who take them.

- Developed countries should encourage their Export Credit Agencies (ECAs) to be more transparent, and to require higher standards of transparency in their support for projects in developing countries. Developed countries should also fully implement the Action Statement on

Bribery and Officially Supported Export Credits agreed by members of the industrialised nations group, the OECD.

- Countries and territories with significant financial centres should take, as a matter of urgency, all necessary legal and administrative measures to repatriate illicitly acquired state funds and assets. We call on G8 countries to make specific commitments in 2005 and to report back on progress, including sums repatriated, in 2006.

- All states should ratify and implement the UN Convention against Corruption during 2005 and should encourage more transparent procurement policies in both Africa and the developed world, particularly in the areas of construction and engineering.

Strengthen information systems

- Good information is essential to informed policy-making and effective delivery. Donors should provide the additional amount required to help Africa improve systems to collect and analyse statistics, to meet criteria normally regarded as an acceptable minimum (estimated at about an additional US$60 million per year).

B: Recommendations on Peace and Security

The right to life and security is the most basic of human rights. Without increased investment in conflict prevention, Africa will not make the rapid acceleration in development that its people seek. Responsibility for resolving conflict in Africa should lie primarily with

Africans, but there is much more the developed world can do to strengthen conflict prevention. Investing in development is itself an investment in peace and security.

Tackling the causes of conflict, and building the capacity to manage them

- To make aid more effective at reducing conflict, all donors, the international financial institutions, and the United Nations should be required to use assessments of how to reduce the risk of violent conflict and improve human security in formulating their country and regional assistance strategies.
- As a matter of priority and no later than 2006, the international community should open negotiations on an international Arms Trade Treaty (ATT).
- The international community must also adopt more effective and legally binding agreements on territorial and extraterritorial arms brokering, and common standards on monitoring and enforcement. These agreements could be integrated into a comprehensive ATT.
- To speed up action to control the trade in natural resources that fund wars, the international community should:
  - agree a common definition of 'conflict resources', for global endorsement through the United Nations;
  - create a permanent Expert Panel within the UN to monitor the links between natural resource extraction and violent conflict and the implementation of sanctions. The panel should be empowered to recommend enforcement measures to the UN Security Council.

• OECD countries should promote the development and full implementation of clear and comprehensive guidelines for companies operating in areas at risk of violent conflict, for incorporation into the OECD Guidelines on Multinational Enterprises.

Building regional and global capacity to prevent and resolve conflict

The international community must honour existing commitments to strengthen African peacekeeping capacity, including support for training and logistics. But it must move beyond this to increase investment in more effective prevention and non-military means to resolve conflict.

• To enable the African Union to act quickly and effectively to prevent and resolve violent conflict, donors should agree to fund at least 50 per cent of the AU's Peace Fund from 2005 onwards. As far as possible, and in return for the implementation of effective financial accountability by the AU, these contributions ought to be unearmarked and provided jointly on an annual basis. Where funds are provided directly to Africa's regional economic communities, these should also be co-ordinated and, where possible, unearmarked.

• In 2005, the UN and regional organisations must take steps to clarify their respective roles and responsibilities, and the criteria for taking action to prevent and resolve conflict. They must also establish effective co-ordination mechanisms.

• In 2005, the UN Security Council should establish the

UN Peacebuilding Commission, as proposed by the United Nations High Level Panel on Threats, Challenges and Change. It should have the powers and resources required to fulfil its mandate to prevent violent conflict, and co-ordinate post-conflict reconstruction.

Post-conflict peacebuilding

As well as supporting the UN Peacebuilding Commission to improve the co-ordination of post-conflict peacebuilding, we recommend further measures:

- Donors should fund the rapid clearance of arrears for post-conflict countries in Africa to enable early access to concessional financing from international financial institutions. In line with this report's recommendations on aid quality, they should also allocate long-term and predictable grant financing sufficient to meet the reconstruction needs of post-conflict countries.

C: Recommendations on Leaving No One Out: Investing in People

There is no substitute for the large increase in resources that are required to reverse years of chronic under-investment in education, health and social protection.

Effective use of these large new resource flows will require comprehensive plans for delivery and for monitoring results. To this end, African governments must continue to strengthen governance and ensure the participation of ordinary people and local communities in decisions on development. For its part, the international community must deliver what it has promised. Both African governments and international donors must ensure that opportunities are available to all.

Education

- Donors and African governments should meet their commitments to achieve Education for All, ensuring that every child in Africa goes to school. Donors should provide an additional US$ 7–8 billion per year as African governments develop comprehensive national plans to deliver quality education.
  - In their national plans African governments must identify measures to get girls as well as boys into school with proper allocation of resources. Donors should meet these additional costs.
  - African governments should undertake to remove school fees for basic education, and donors should fund this until countries can afford these costs themselves.
  - To ensure that high-quality education is delivered, African governments must invest in teacher training, retention of staff and professional development. Teacher/child ratios should be brought to under 1:40 in basic education. Donors should commit to predictable long-term funding to enable this.
  - Education should provide relevant skills for contemporary Africa. Donors should fund regional networks to support African governments in the development of more appropriate curricula at all levels.

Health

- African governments should invest in rebuilding systems to deliver public health services. Donors should provide US$7 billion over five years for this, behind the Health Strategy and Initial Programme of Action of the African Union's NEPAD Programme.
- Donors and African governments should urgently invest in training and retention to ensure there are an additional one million health workers by 2015.
- African governments should meet their commitment to allocate 15 per cent of annual budgets to health and put in place strategies for the effective delivery of health services. Donors should increase their funding to support these strategies, making up the shortfall, from an additional US$10 billion annually immediately and rising to US$20 billion annually by 2015. The assistance should go predominantly through national budgets.
  - Where African governments remove fees for basic healthcare as part of reform, donors should make a long-term commitment to fill the financing gap until countries can take on these costs.
  - Donors should fully fund the Global Fund to Fight AIDS, Tuberculosis and Malaria.
  - Donors should commit to full funding of the Global Alliance for Vaccines and Immunisation (GAVI) through the International Financing Facility for Immunisation. They should also meet their commitments to the Polio Eradication Initiative to eradicate polio in 2005.
  - The World Health Organisation's 'Two diseases, one patient' strategy should be supported to provide integrated TB and HIV care.

- African governments and donors should work together to ensure that every pregnant mother and every child has a long-lasting insecticide-treated net and is provided with effective malaria drugs.
- Donors should ensure that there is adequate funding for the treatment and prevention of parasitic diseases and micronutrient deficiency. Governments and global health partnerships should ensure that this is integrated into public health campaigns by 2006.
- African governments must show strong leadership in promoting women's and men's right to sexual and reproductive health. Donors should do all they can to enable universal access to sexual and reproductive health services.
- Donors should develop incentives for research and development in health that meet Africa's needs. They must set up advance purchase agreements for medicines. They should increase direct funding of research led by Africa, co-ordinated by the Regional Economic Communities and in collaboration with the global health partnerships.

Water and sanitation

- Starting in 2005, donors must reverse the decline in aid for water supply and sanitation, to enable African governments to achieve the Africa Water Vision commitment to reduce by 75 per cent the proportion of people without access to safe water and sanitation by 2015. The G8 should report back by 2007 on implementation of the G8 Water Action Plan agreed in 2003.

HIV and AIDS

- The international community must reach a global agreement in 2005 to harmonise the current disparate response to HIV and AIDS. This must be in support of bold and comprehensive strategies by African governments that take account of power relationships between men, women and young people.

- As agreed in the UNGASS Declaration of Commitment on HIV and AIDS, African governments and the international community should work together urgently to deliver the right of people to prevention, treatment and care. Donors should meet the immediate needs and increase their contribution by at least US$10 billion annually within five years.

Protecting the most vulnerable

- African governments should develop social protection strategies for orphans and vulnerable children, by supporting their extended families and communities. Donors should commit to long-term, predictable funding of these strategies with US$2 billion a year immediately, rising to US$5 to 6 billion a year by 2015.
  - Donors should support the African Union's NEPAD Programme to develop a rights and inclusion framework and support countries to develop social protection strategies by 2007.
  - Donors and African governments should endorse and implement the UN Framework for the Protection, Care and Support of the Orphans and Vulnerable Children.

- Donors and African governments should provide direct budgetary support to pan-African organisations to support their work in protecting women and children's rights.

D: Recommendations on Growth and Poverty Reduction

Poverty in Africa will continue to rise unless there is greater economic growth – and of a kind in which poor people can participate. And none should be excluded. Policy-makers must always consider the impact of policies on poor people. The package of proposals set out in this and other chapters should enable sub-Saharan African countries to achieve and sustain growth rates of seven per cent by 2010. They will also boost the participation of poor people in the opportunities created by growth. In so doing they will work to reduce income inequality, which can undermine the impact of growth on poverty.

Our proposals here are divided in two. The first set relates primarily to promoting growth. Faster growth and greater poverty reduction require major investment in infrastructure, agriculture, urban development, the creation of a climate which fosters investment, and policies which take careful account of the environment and climate change. Growth will be driven by the private sector, but government creates the conditions for this – the challenge is to build a strong partnership.

The second set of proposals relates to promoting

poor people's participation in that growth. In this, particular emphasis should be placed on much stronger opportunities and rights for women, who are often key to small enterprise growth. Young people need job opportunities. The business community can also play a part in these areas.

Promoting growth

Africa needs an additional US$20 billion a year investment in infrastructure. To support this, developed countries should provide an extra US$10 billion a year up to 2010 and, subject to review, a further increase to US$20 billion a year in the following five years. This should support African regional, national, urban and rural infrastructure priorities – ranging from rural roads and slum upgrading to information and communication technology and the infrastructure needed to support greater integration of Africa's regions and to enable Africa to break into world markets.

African governments must unleash the strong entrepreneurial spirit of Africa's people. To promote this, donor governments and the private sector should coordinate their efforts behind the proposed Investment Climate Facility of the African Union's NEPAD Programme. This requires US$550 million from donors and the private sector over seven years to identify and overcome the obstacles to doing business. In addition, developed countries should support a fund of the Multilateral Investment Guarantee Agency, the world's public agency for risk-bearing, to insure foreign and domestic investors in post-conflict countries in Africa.

Support should also be extended to domestic investors across sub-Saharan Africa.

As part of a wider set of measures to promote agricultural and rural development, Africa must double the area of arable land under irrigation by 2015. Donors should support this, initially focusing on funding a 50 per cent increase by 2010, with an emphasis on small-scale irrigation. Other measures include improving the investment climate; rural infrastructure; research and the spread of new agricultural techniques; security of tenure and land rights, particularly for women; and investment in small towns to encourage the growth of local and regional markets.

Poor people's participation in growth

Developed countries should set up a US$100 million Africa Enterprise Challenge Fund to support private sector initiatives that contribute to small enterprise development by giving them better access to markets. The Fund will encourage new partnerships in the financial and non-financial sectors and contribute to the African Union's objectives of promoting job creation for young people and women's entrepreneurship.

African governments must take the lead in promoting employment for young people, both women and men, in their policies for growth. Donors should assist African governments in formulating and implementing national action plans on employment through the Youth Employment Network, as endorsed by the African Union.

Promoting the role of business

The Commission calls for a sea change in the way the business community, both domestic and international, engages in the development process in Africa. Businesses must sign up to leading codes of good social and environmental conduct, including on corruption and transparency, and focus their efforts on co-ordinated action to tackle poverty – working in partnership with each other, with donors, with national governments, and with civil society, including trades unions. In support of this, developed countries should support the UNDP Growing Sustainable Business initiative in the region. For their part, donors and African governments must develop more effective partnerships with the private sector.

The environment and climate change

In support of the Environment Initiative of the African Union's NEPAD Programme, donors should strengthen environmental considerations in all their programmes. Donor governments and international institutions, including the World Bank, the UN Environment Programme (UNEP) and the UN Development Programme (UNDP), should encourage the inclusion of environmental sustainability in African government's poverty reduction strategies. These should include indicators for monitoring environmental performance.

Developed countries should set targets for greater use of new cleaner energy technologies to stimulate the global market and encourage their use in developing countries. Donors should work to improve the climate observation network through the Global Climate Observation System, bilateral support, and a co-ordinated capacity building programme between donor and African research institutions. From 2008, donors should make climate variability and climate change risk factors an integral part of their project planning and assessment. They should meet their commitments on funding to help African countries adapt to the risks and impacts of climate change.

E: Recommendations on Trade

Increased trade is vital to increased growth. Africa's share of world trade has slumped to just two per cent from six per cent twenty years ago, and Africa has fallen behind its competitors. Africa faces a huge challenge if it is to reverse this and catch up. African govern-ments must drive this process and be allowed to develop their own trade policies. Action in three key areas by African countries and the international community, working together, could make this happen by: support-ing African-owned strategies for building the capacity to trade; dismantling the rich world's trade barriers through the Doha Round of world trade negotiations; and providing transitional support to help Africa adjust to new trading regimes.

Improving Africa's capacity to trade

- Africa must increase its capacity to trade. It should remove its own internal trade barriers between one African country and another. Measures to facilitate trade will be key, including reform of customs and other regulations. And it must increase efforts to achieve greater economic efficiency through integration and increased co-operation within African regions. Some of these steps will be relatively easy and low-cost.

- Africa should do more to improve the economic environment for farmers and firms, backed up by major investments of aid from international donors to ensure Africa can produce and trade competitively. Funding for infrastructure should, in part, be spent on improving African transport and communications to bring down costs.

Improving Africa's access to the markets of the rich world

- Developed countries should ensure the Doha Round of world trade talks makes development its absolute priority at the December 2005 meetings of the WTO in Hong Kong. The Doha talks should conclude no later than the end of 2006 in order to make an early difference to Africa and other developing countries.

- Rich countries must agree to eliminate immediately trade-distorting support to cotton and sugar, and commit by 2010 to end all export subsidies and all trade-distorting support in agriculture when they meet in Hong Kong. At the conclusion of the Doha talks they should agree to reduce progressively all tariffs to zero by 2015, and reduce non-tariff barriers. By doing this they will cut massive wasteful spending, and provide huge benefits to their own public, and to Africa and other developing countries.

- Higher-income developing countries should also do more to reduce their tariffs and other barriers to trade with Africa.

- In making development a priority in trade talks, including in the new trade agreements Europe is currently negotiating with Africa, liberalisation must not be forced on Africa through trade or aid conditions and must be done in a way that reduces reciprocal demands to a minimum. Individual African countries should be allowed to sequence their own trade reforms, at their own pace, in line with their own poverty reduction and development plans. Additional financial assistance should be provided to support developing countries in building the capacity they need to trade and adjust to more open markets.

- Special and Differential Treatment must be made to work better for Africa and other developing countries, by making resort to legal disputes conditional on assessing development concerns. A review of Article XXIV of the General Agreement on Tariffs and Trade in order to reduce requirements for reciprocity and increase focus on development priorities may be useful.

- Although Africa wants to meet developed country product standards, it is struggling to meet the costs of doing so. Rich countries should apply a development test, including an impact assessment, when designing these standards, to minimise the barriers they may create, and urgently provide help to meet them.

Helping Africa adjust to new trade regimes

It will take time to build Africa's capacity to trade, and to deliver reform in the Doha Round. During this period, Africa will need transitional support if it is to make progress.

- Developed countries should remove all barriers to all exports from low-income sub-Saharan countries, by extending quota and duty-free access to all of them. This will cost developed countries very little. They should cease to apply rules-of-origin requirements in a way designed to hinder rather than help African exporters, by allowing Africa to source inputs from anywhere in the world, and requiring only that they add a minimum of 10 per cent of value in their processing. Europe's new trade agreements with Africa must move quickly on this. If all developed countries extended quota and duty-free access to all low-income sub-Saharan African countries this could raise annual incomes in sub-Saharan Africa by up to US$5 billion.
- Rich countries should also provide aid to help African economies adjust to a more open global trade regime, and to enhance the benefits to and limit the detrimental impacts on poor people.

F: Recommendations on Resources

To increase the growth rate in Africa, and to make strong progress towards the Millennium Development Goals, the volume and quality of external aid to sub-Saharan Africa must change radically. Aid to sub-Saharan Africa should increase by US$25 billion per annum over the next three to five years. This must be accompanied by a radical change in the way donors behave and deliver assistance, and by continued strong improvements in governance in African countries. We show that in these circumstances this increase in aid can be used effectively. Additional finance should be raised in various ways, including the immediate launch of the International Finance Facility.

Aid quality

- To improve the quality of aid an annual discussion should take place between the Development Ministers of the OECD countries and African Finance Ministers, along with representatives of civil society and international organisations. This should consider aid allocation criteria and make suggestions for a better distribution, including between middle- and low-income countries. In countries where governance and institutions are weaker, donors should seek to provide adequate and effective flows through appropriate channels, bearing in mind the need to avoid undermining national systems and/or long-term sustainability.
- Aid should be untied, predictable, harmonised, and linked to the decision-making and budget processes of the country receiving it. The length of the commitment should be related to the purpose: for example, aid for infrastructure and public expenditure support should be committed for terms longer than aid for technical assistance.
- Aid to Africa should be mainly in the form of grants.

- The use of policy conditionality associated with external assistance should be strongly reduced. Ways of strengthening mutual accountability, and of monitoring implementation, should be put in place. The activities of the international financial institutions and donors should support and not undermine institutions of accountability in African countries, for example by helping countries to strengthen international codes and standards and by avoiding heavy burdens of reporting.
- Through a new facility, donors should help African countries to address problems caused by commodity-related shocks and natural disasters.

Aid quantity

- Aid to sub-Saharan Africa should be doubled, that is, increased by US$25 billion per annum, over the next three to five years to complement rising levels of domestic revenue arising from growth and from better governance. Following a review of progress towards the end of this period, a further US$25 billion per annum should be provided, building on changes in the qualiy of aid and improvements in governance.

Debt relief

- For poor countries in sub-Saharan Africa which need it, the objective must be 100 per cent debt cancellation as soon as possible. This must be part of a financing package for these countries to achieve the Millennium Development Goals, as promised in Monterrey and Kananaskis. The key criterion should be that the money be used to deliver development, economic growth and the reduction of poverty for countries actively promoting good governance.

- Accordingly, work should begin immediately to establish a transparent debt compact to include all sub-Saharan African low-income countries, including those excluded from current schemes. It should cancel debt stock and debt service by up to 100 per cent, and cover multilateral and bilateral debt.
- As an urgent measure, financing should immediately be put in place to provide 100 per cent multilateral debt service cancellation, where this is necessary to achieve the MDGs.

Financing mechanisms

- Donor countries should commit immediately to their fair share of the additional US$25 billion per annum necessary for Africa.
- Ways of financing the doubling of aid to Africa should include the immediate launch of the International Finance Facility.
- Rich countries should aim to spend 0.7 per cent of their annual income on aid, with plans specified for meeting this target.
- Further work should be undertaken to develop workable proposals for specific international levies to raise additional finance (for example from compulsory or voluntary charges on airline tickets).

G: *Recommendations on How to Make All This Happen*

If Africa is to take responsibility for its own development, it must be given greater influence in decision-making which affects it most directly. It must have a stronger voice in international forums. And it must be able to exert much greater pressure on the rich world to honour its commitments to the poor people of Africa. An independent monitoring system must be established to make sure this happens.

Strengthening the African multilateral institutions

- Shareholders of the African Development Bank should aim to make the African Development Bank the pre-eminent financing institution in Africa within 10 years. Proposals should be put forward by the new president within six months of taking office. Shareholders should provide strong support for their implementation.
- Strong support should be provided for the further enhancement of the role of the Economic Commission for Africa.

Changing the multilateral organisations

STRATEGY
- The management of the World Bank, the IMF, and the WTO should give greater priority to accelerating Africa's development. Proposals to do so should be presented to the Boards of Governors of the World Bank and IMF

(preferably at the 2005 Annual Meetings of the two institutions, but certainly no later than the 2006 Spring Meetings) and the WTO's 2005 Ministerial.

- The UN Secretary General and the UN Development Group should strengthen the co-ordination of UN agencies, funds and programmes at country level, to improve their impact.

VOICE

- African countries should be given a greater voice in the multilateral institutions, most notably through greater representation on the boards of the World Bank and IMF.
- Strategic leadership and decision-making in the IMF and World Bank must be the responsibility of the political leadership of member countries. To this end, a decision-making Council, consisting of political representatives of member countries, should be established for each institution.
- Appointments of the heads of international institutions should be decided upon by open competition which looks for the best candidate rather than by traditions which limit these appointments by nationality.
- In each recipient country, the government and donors should set up monitoring groups to assess the quality of donor assistance and co-ordination.
- The UN Security Council should be expanded to include greater African representation.

Putting in place effective independent monitoring mechanisms

- To add extra momentum to the delivery of the Commission's recommendations, an independent mechanism, which reflects the consultative approach of the Commission, should be established to monitor and report on progress. This could be led by two distinguished and influential figures who carry weight in the international community, one African and one from the donor community, who could produce a short annual report. They should be supported by a small unit within an existing African or international institution.

Abbreviations

AIDS	Acquired Immune Deficiency Syndrome
ATT	Arms Trade Treaty
AU	African Union
EITI	Extractive Industries Transparency Initiative
EU	European Union
GAVI	Global Alliance for Vaccines and Immunisation
HIPC	Heavily Indebted Poor Countries
HIV	Human Immunodeficiency Virus
IFF	International Finance Facility
IMF	International Monetary Fund
MDG	Millennium Development Goal
MFI	Micro-Finance Institutions
NEPAD	New Partnership for Africa's Development
OECD	Organisation for Economic Co-operation and Development
TB	Tuberculosis
UK	United Kingdom
UN	United Nations
UNDP	United Nations Development Program
UNEP	United Nations Environment Program
UNGASS	United Nations General Assembly Special Session
WTO	World Trade Organisation

Glossary

0.7 per cent

The level of Gross National Income (GNI) that rich countries should make available for Official Development Assistance (ODA) to developing countries, as recommended by the Pearson Commission in 1970. By 2003, only five donors had reached that target: Denmark, Luxembourg, The Netherlands, Norway and Sweden. Recently, Finland, Spain, the UK, France and Belgium announced timetables to reach this target.

African Development Bank (ADB)

A regional multilateral development bank, engaged in promoting the economic development and social progress of its Regional Member Countries in Africa. Its shareholders are 53 countries in Africa as well as 24 countries in the Americas, Europe, and Asia. It was established in 1964 with headquarters in Abidjan, Côte d'Ivoire, although it currently operates out of Tunis due to instability in Côte d'Ivoire.

African Peer Review Mechanism (APRM)

A voluntary system launched in 2002 and open to all members of the African Union (see below), designed to promote the adoption of agreed governance standards. To accede to the APRM, a state must sign the 2002 NEPAD (see below) Declaration on Democracy, Political, Economic and Corporate Governance, and undertake to submit to periodic peer reviews. The first four reviews are underway.

African Union (AU)

The successor organisation to the Organisation for African Unity (OAU), the AU was established in 2002. The AU works to promote African economic, social and political integration as well as peace and security. Its headquarters are in Addis Ababa, Ethiopia. When fully realised, the AU will have a General Assembly, Executive Council, Pan-African Parliament (established in 2004), African Central Bank (and eventual common currency), African Monetary Fund, and other organs and agencies.

Arms brokering

The arrangement and facilitation of arms transfers between suppliers and purchasers who may be, but are not necessarily, outside the country. Arms brokering can cover a range of activities from setting up deals to arranging transport facilities and cargo clearance for arms. Arms brokers will typically benefit materially without necessarily taking possession or ownership of the goods they are involved in transferring.

Basic education

UNESCO (2004) defines basic education as the 'whole range of educational activities, taking place in various settings, that aim to meet basic learning needs as defined in the World Declaration on Education for All [Jomtien, Thailand, 1990]. According to the International Standard Classification of Education (ISCED), basic education comprises primary education [first stage of basic education] and lower secondary education [second stage]. It also covers a wide variety of non-formal and informal public and private activities intended to meet the basic learning needs of people of all ages. AU/NEPAD defines basic education as a nine-year cycle.'

Booty futures

Advance rights to extract resources in areas that rebels hope to capture during war. Rebels sell these rights to raise finance to fund their offensive. Unique to Africa, booty futures have been used to initiate at least one, and prolong at least three armed struggles.

Brandt Commission

An independent commission on international development set up in 1977 by World Bank president Robert McNamara. Headed by former German Chancellor Willy Brandt, the Commission's purpose was to influence public opinion to help change government attitudes, as well as to make proposals for revitalising negotiations between the countries of the North (rich countries) and the South around global development. It produced two influential reports, *North-South* (1980) and *Common Crisis* (1983).

Capacity

The ability of individuals, organisations and societies to perform functions, solve problems and set and achieve their own objectives. In a development context, 'capacity development' refers to investment in people, institutions, and practices that will, together, enable that country to achieve its development objectives (World Bank, 1997).

Challenge fund

A challenge fund is a public financing mechanism that allocates grant funding through a competitive process. Challenge funds are set up to meet specific objectives – such as extending financial services to poor people. It is up to bidders to propose innovative ways of achieving the fund's objectives. Bids are assessed against transparent criteria, and successful bidders must match (or more than match) the grant amount. In this way, the public sector shares some of the initial risks associated with investments.

Civil society

All those social organisations outside the state, the family and the market: business associations, employers' associations, trades unions, charities, community groups, professional associations, women's organisations, advocacy groups, church and faith groups, trade associations, self-help groups, recreational groups, media, academia and so on.

Coltan

Coltan (short for Colombite-Tantalite) is a metallic ore, which is found mainly in the Eastern Democratic Republic of Congo. When it is refined, coltan produces metallic tantalum, which can store high electric charges and is therefore used in capacitators. These are commonly used, for example, in mobile telephones.

Comparative advantage

The ability to produce a good at lower cost, relative to other goods, compared to another country.

Debt service

The sum of principal repayments and interest actually paid in foreign currency, goods or services on long-term debt, plus interest paid on short-term debt (i.e. debt which is due within one year).

Economic Commission for Africa (ECA)

Established in 1958, one of five regional commissions under the administrative direction of United Nations (UN) headquarters, mandated to support the economic and social development of its 53 member states, foster regional integration, and promote international co-operation for Africa's development.

Economic growth

The annual increase in a nation's total output of goods and services or the annual increase in the nation's total income.

Education for All

Education for All dates to the Jomtien Conference in 1990. In 2000, countries reiterated their commitment and set six goals in the Dakar Framework for Action (2000) on early childhood care and education, youth and adult learning, gender, universal primary education, literacy and quality.

European Union (EU)

The European Union is made up of 25 member states. Common institutions, including the Council of the European Union, the European Parliament and the European Commission, take decisions on and manage specific matters of joint interest at European level.

Exclusion

Denial of entitlements or access to decision-making processes and services, including the justice system for certain groups. Exclusion is often on the basis of a person's identity, for example, as a woman or as a part of an ethnic group.

Extraterritorial arms brokering

Arms brokers operating from outside their country of residence or nationality.

Fast-track Initiative (FTI)

Launched in June 2002 as a practical response to the commitment to Education for All to mobilise increased and better co-ordinated resources for those low-income countries making serious efforts to improve primary education. Designed on the principles of the Monterrey Consensus, the FTI is built on mutual accountability whereby increased donor support for primary education is based on a country's policy performance and accountability for results.

G8

The G7 plus the Russian Federation.

General Agreement on Tariffs and Trade (GATT)

The GATT is the founding basis of the WTO and covers regulation related to trade in goods. The GATT is the overriding framework within which other agreements – such as agriculture and SPS etc. – fit. GATT came into being in 1947.

Global Health Partnerships

International coalitions to tackle a single disease or group of diseases.

Heavily Indebted Poor Countries (HIPC)

The HIPC Initiative was first launched in 1996 by the IMF and World Bank. Its aim is to reduce the excessive debt burdens faced by the world's poorest nations. The Initiative entails co-ordinated action by the international financial community, including multilateral organisations and governments, to reduce to sustainable levels the external debt burdens of the most heavily indebted poor countries. The HIPC Initiative currently identifies 38 countries, 32 of them in sub-Saharan Africa, as potentially eligible to receive debt relief.

Humanitarian assistance

Temporary assistance designed to rapidly reduce human suffering, including 'objects indispensable to the survival of the civilian population (including food supplies, crops, livestock, water, water installations and irrigation works, medicine, objects necessary for religious worship, clothing, beddings, and shelter)'.

Human security

People-centred 'human security becomes an all-encompassing condition in which individual citizens live in freedom, peace and safety and participate fully in the process of governance. They enjoy the protection of fundamental rights, have access to resources and the basic necessities of life, including health and education, and inhabit an environment that is not injurious to their health and well-being.'

Informal economy

Conceptually, the informal economy stands in opposition to the 'formal' economy, i.e. that part of the economy whose activities are recorded in national accounts and operate under rules and regulations imposed by the government. By contrast, economic activities in the informal sector are not recorded in national accounts (hence often called 'invisible') and are not subject to formal rules of contract, licensing, labour laws, reporting and taxation (ILO, 1984). The quality of information about the size, magnitude and composition of the informal economy in Africa is generally very poor.

Infrastructure

Economic infrastructure including energy, transport, information and communication technology, water supply and sanitation and other water resource infrastructure and social infrastructure, such as schools and health centres.

Investment climate

The investment climate consists of the local factors that shape the opportunities and incentives for firms to invest productively, create jobs and expand. Government policies and behaviours play a critical role by affecting the costs, risk and barriers to competition faced by firms. Important issues identified in studies and business surveys include: policy predictability; macroeconomic stability; good provision of health, education and infrastructure services; the quality and accountability of public financial management systems; the predictability and transparency of taxation; the nature of business regulation; the level of corruption; an effective and fair judiciary; well-implemented competition laws; efficient financial markets; and political instability, conflict and crime.

International Finance Facility (IFF)

Launched in January 2003 by the UK's HM Treasury and DFID, the IFF is a financing mechanism designed to substantially increase development financing in the short run. It would leverage in additional money from the international capital markets by issuing bonds, based on legally binding long-term donor commitments. Participating donor countries would be responsible for repaying bondholders using future donor aid streams.

International Monetary Fund (IMF)

The IMF has 184 members and works to foster global monetary co-operation, secure financial stability, facilitate international trade, promote high employment and sustainable economic growth, and reduce poverty.

Kimberley Process

An initiative in which governments, industry and NGOs joined together to stem the flow of so-called 'conflict diamonds' – rough diamonds that have been used to finance wars and that have mostly been obtained or traded illicitly. The Kimberley Process Certification Scheme is a voluntary system that imposes extensive requirements on participants to certify that shipments of rough diamonds are free from conflict diamonds. It accounts for approximately 98 per cent of the world trade in rough diamonds.

Micro-finance

The provision of financial services to poor people, including small-scale credit, savings, deposits, insurance services and pro-poor mortgage mechanisms.

Millennium Development Goals (MDGs)

At the UN General Assembly in 2000, governments committed to achieving the following goals by 2015: eradicating extreme poverty and hunger, achieving primary education, promoting gender equality and empowering women, reducing child mortality, improving maternal health, combating HIV and AIDS, malaria, and other disease, ensuring environmental sustainability, and developing a global partnership for development.

Multilateral Investment Guarantee Agency (MIGA)

MIGA, part of the World Bank Group, is a global insurer to private investors and adviser to countries on foreign investment. It aims to promote foreign direct investment into developing countries in support of growth and poverty reduction.

The New Partnership for Africa's Development (NEPAD)

NEPAD is a programme of the AU and was adopted at the 37th session of the Assembly of Heads of State and Government in July 2001. It seeks to strengthen peace, security, economic and political governance, and regional integration.

Non-governmental organisation (NGO)

An organisation that is not part of a government. NGOs are usually not-for-profit organisations. See also 'civil society'.

Organisation for African Unity (OAU)

The Organisation of African Unity (OAU) was established in May 1963. It aimed to promote the unity and solidarity of the African states and act as a collective voice for the continent. It was succeeded in July 2002 by the African Union.

Organisation for Economic Co-operation and Development (OECD)

A group of major industrial countries promoting growth and high employment among its members, fostering international trade and contributing to global economic development.

Peacebuilding

'Activities that are focused on long-term support to, and establishment of, viable political, socio-economic and cultural institutions capable of addressing the root causes of conflicts and mediating social conflict, as well as other initiatives aimed at creating the necessary conditions for sustained peace and stability. These activities also seek to promote the integration of competing or marginalised groups within mainstream society, through providing equitable access to political decision-making, social networks, economic resources and information and can be implemented in all phases of conflict'.

Peacekeeping (peace support operations)

The UN 'Agenda for Peace' defines peacekeeping as the deployment of a United Nations presence in the field, hitherto with the consent of all the parties concerned, normally involving United Nations military and/or police personnel and frequently civilians as well. Peacekeeping is a technique that expands the possibilities for both the prevention of conflict and the making of peace.' For the purpose of this report we use peacekeeping as a generic term that encompasses the whole range of military and civilian deployment into a conflict zone with or without the consent of all the parties including peacekeeping, peace enforcement, peacebuilding/making and preventive diplomacy. Some countries/organisations also use the term 'peace support operations'.

Poverty Reduction Strategy (PRS)

Initiated by the boards of the World Bank and International Monetary Fund (IMF), a poverty reduction strategy should describe a country's macroeconomic, structural and social policies and programmes to promote growth and reduce poverty, as well as associated external financing needs. PRSs are expected to be prepared by governments through a participatory process involving civil society and development partners, including the World Bank and IMF, and are required for countries seeking to obtain concessional lending and debt relief under the enhanced Heavily Indebted Poor Countries (HIPC) initiative.

Project Implementation Units (PIUs)

Project Implementation Units are often autonomous units that administer development assistance programmes. They have been set up when existing civil service staff either do not have the capacity to take on additional tasks, or do not have the technical skills to administer such programmes.

Regional Economic Communities (RECs)

Multilateral African organisations which each serve one or more of Africa's regions: North Africa, East Africa, West Africa, Central Africa and Southern Africa.

Sector-Wide Approach (SWAP)

A SWAP synthesises all policy perspectives within a sector, presents a co-ordinated policy for all the sector activities and guides all spending in the sector (government, donor, private and NGOs) through one strategy.

Tariff

A tax imposed on imports by a government. A tariff may be either a fixed charge per unit of product imported (specific tariff) or a fixed percentage of value (*ad valorem* tariff).

Trade Liberalisation

Reduction of tariffs and removal or relaxation of non-tariff barriers.

UN Convention Against Corruption (UNCAC)

An international treaty negotiated between 2001 and 2003, and opened for signature in December 2003, under the auspices of the United Nations Office on Drugs and Crime, setting global standards for governments in combating corruption. The principal sections cover preventive measures; the offences that should be criminalised; international co-operation, including on repatriation of stolen assets; technical assistance, and follow-up.

UN-HABITAT

The United Nations Human Settlements Programme. The mission of UN-HABITAT is to promote sustainable urbanisation through policy formulation, institutional reform, capacity-building, technical co-operation and advocacy, and to monitor and improve the state of human settlements worldwide.

User fees

A fee charged to those using public goods or services such as health, education, water and other infrastructure services.

Vulnerability

Susceptibility to poverty, hunger, and destitution as a consequence of crisis, because of inability to access services or call on informal support.

World Bank (Group)

Frequently used shorthand for the International Bank for Reconstruction and Development (IBRD), one of the original Bretton Woods institutions. The World Bank Group consists of the IBRD, as well as the International Development Association (IDA); the International Finance Corporation (IFC); the Multilateral Investment Guarantee Agency (MIGA); and the International Centre for the Settlement of Investment Disputes (ICSID).

World Trade Organisation (WTO)

Established on 1 January 1995, as a result of the Uruguay Round, the WTO replaced GATT as the legal and institutional foundation of the multilateral trading system of member countries. It sets forth the principal contractual obligations determining how governments frame and implement domestic trade legislation and regulations. It is also the platform on which trade relations among countries evolve through collective debate and negotiation.

Appendix

More about the work of the Commission for Africa

In this book you have read the first part, (the Argument), and the Recommendations of 'Our Common Interest', the report of the Commission for Africa.

As explained in the introduction, the full report includes an extensive second part, which is the Analysis and Evidence. That part includes full references and sources for the material in this book, as well as the substance and basis necessary for the Commission's work to be held up to public scrutiny.

The full report is available free to download in English and French from the Commission website www.commission forafrica.org, and may be ordered as a single volume from the website. The website also includes full details of the Commission's work, including the extensive consultations and submissions received during the preparation of the report, details of the Commissioners' meetings, background papers and other material.

As additional resources, in the following pages we present the Declaration of the Commission for Africa, which accompanied the publication of the report on 11 March 2005 and a brief guide to the second part of the report, including suggestions for further reading.

I. The Declaration of the Commission for Africa, 11 March 2005

The Commission for Africa finds the condition of the lives of the majority of Africans to be intolerable and an affront to the dignity of all mankind. We insist upon an alteration of these conditions through a change of policy in favour of the weak.

Having analysed and costed how this may be achieved, we call for our conclusions to be implemented forthwith in the cause of right and justice and in the name of our shared humanity.

On the edge of this new century, in an age of unprecedented wealth and economic progress by all continents, it is unacceptable that Africa drifts further from the rest of the world, unseen in its misery and ignored in its pain.

The Commission, its members acting in their capacity as individuals, has assimilated the analysis of years and all extant reports into our findings. These clearly show how things may have been otherwise.

However we exist in contemporary realities. The world is vastly different to that of 20 years ago when we forcefully acknowledged the pity of the Great African Famine of 1984–85. The world, then locked into its Cold War political stasis, remained rigid in its competitive ideologies. The breaking of this deadlock, and the increase in global trade that followed, allied to new technologies and cultural shifts, have created a more fluid, less predictive yet more interdependent world.

This world in flux has brought great opportunities along with confusion, change and anxiety. But such change poses great possibilities for us all and especially for Africa, that great giant finally beginning to stir itself from its enforced slumber. We need, then, to seek to understand these newer forces in play about us, attempt to define them and in so doing set the framework for policies that favour the poor.

The great nations of the world, in alliance with their African neighbours, must now move together, in our common interest. How they may proceed will be determined by each nation's needs and desires. But all must immediately begin the journey that leads us to the ultimate common destination of a more equitable world.

Our task was the first step. It is done.

11 March 2005

II. Guide to the Analysis and Evidence in the full report of the Commission for Africa, and suggestions for further reading

The second part of the Commission's report, the Analysis and Evidence, is made up of 10 chapters, each corresponding to the chapters of the Argument presented in this book. Chapters 1–3 set out the structure of the report. Chapters 4 to 10 cover the policy areas in the Commission's recommendations. Those chapters and the references contained in them should be the primary source for those interested in the full range of the Commission's work. The submissions to the Commission's consultations, which are published on the Commission website, are another point of reference. As an additional resource, some of the principal text sources for each chapter are summarised here as other suggestions for further reading.

Chapter 3. *Through African eyes*

The Committee on African Studies (2004) *Harvard Africa Initiative,* Working Paper, Harvard University.

Ellis, S and G Ter Haar (2004) *Worlds of Power: Religious Thought and Political Practice,* New York: OUP.

New Partnership for Africa's Development (NEPAD) (2001) Base Document. Available at www.nepad.org

Rao, V and M Walton (eds) (2004) *Culture and Public Action,* Stanford University Press.

Reports and papers from Bob Geldof's series of new thinking seminars in Berlin, London, Rome, Paris and New York (2004), www.commissionforafrica.org

Tibaijuka, A (2005) *Africa on the move: an urban crisis in the making,* paper prepared for the Commission for Africa: UN-HABITAT. Available at www.commissionforafrica.org

United Nations Development Programme (UNDP) (2004) *Human Development Report 2004: Cultural liberty in today's diverse world,* New York: UNDP.

Chapter 4. *Getting systems right: governance and capacity-building*

Bennell P (2004) *Teacher Motivation and Incentives in sub-Saharan Africa and Asia, Knowledge and Skills for Development,* Brighton.

Economic Commission for Africa (2004) *Striving for Good Governance in Africa*, Synopsis of the 2005 Africa Governance Report Prepared for the African Development Forum IV, Economic Commission for Africa.

Gary, I and T L Karl (2003) *Bottom of the Barrel: Africa's Oil Boom and the Poor*, Catholic Relief Services, accessed via http://www.catholicrelief.org/get_involved/advocacy/policy_and_strategic_issues/oil_report_full.pdf

Levy, B and S Kpundeh (eds) (2004) *Building State Capacity in Africa: New Approaches and Emerging Lessons*, World Bank Institute, Washington DC: World Bank.

Ndulu, B (2004) *Human Capital Flight: Stratification, Globalization and the Challenges to Tertiary Education in Africa*, Washington DC: World Bank.

Sawyerr, A (2004) *Challenges Facing African Universities, Selected Issues*, African Association of Universities, accessed via: http://aau.org/english/documents/asachallenges.pdf

Transparency International (2004) *Global Corruption Report 2004*, accessed via http://www.globalcorruptionreport.org

UNCTAD (2003) *Commodity Yearbook Vols I and II*, United Nations Conference on Trade and Development, accessed via http://www.unctad.org/en/docs/tdbcn1stat4vol1_enfr.pdf

World Bank (2004) *Striking a Better Balance: the World Bank and Extractive Industries. The Final Report of the Extractive Industries Review – World Bank Group Management Response*, accessed via http://www.worldbank.org/ogmc/files/finaleirmanagementresponseexecsum.pdf

Chapter 5. The need for peace and security

Chalmers, M and S Willett (2003) *Spending to Save? An Analysis of the Cost Effectiveness of Conflict Prevention Versus Intervention after the Onset of Violent Conflict: Phase 1 Final Report*, Bradford: Centre for International Co-operation and Security, Department of Peace Studies, University of Bradford.

Collier, P et al. (2003) *Breaking the Conflict Trap: Civil War and Development Policy*, World Bank report, Oxford: Oxford University Press.

Cross, P, C Flew and A McLean (2004) *Evidence and Analysis: Tackling the Availability and Misuse of Small Arms in Africa*, background paper prepared for the Commission for Africa.

Faria, F (2004) *Crisis Management in Sub-Saharan Africa: The Role of the European Union*, Paris: EU Institute for Security Studies.

Lunde, L and M Taylor, with A Huser (2003) *Commerce or Crime? Regulating Economies of Conflict*, Fafo-Report 424, Programme for International Co-operation and Conflict Resolution, Oslo: Fafo Institute for Applied Social Science.

Nathan, L (2004) *'The Four Horsemen of the Apocalypse': the Structural Causes of Crisis and Violence in Africa*, paper for the Crisis States Programme, Development Studies Institute, London School of Economics and Political Science.

OECD Watch (2004) *The OECD Guidelines for Multinational Enterprises and Supply Chain Responsibility: A*

Discussion Paper, accessed via http://www.bsl.org.au/pdfs/OECD_Watch_supply_chain_discussion_paper.pdf

Ross, M (2003) *Natural Resources and Civil War: An Overview,* report for the conference on 'The Governance of Natural Resources Revenues', World Bank/PFD, Paris, December 9–10, 2002.

Stevens, P (2003) *Resource Impact: Curse or Blessing?* A Literature Survey. IPIECA, Centre for Energy, Petroleum and Mineral Law and Policy, Dundee: University of Dundee.

United Nations High-Level Panel on Threats, Challenges and Change (2004) *A More Secure World: Our Shared Responsibility: Report of the High-level Panel on Threats, Challenges and Change,* New York: United Nations.

Chapter 6. Leaving no one out: investing in people

General reading

UNICEF (2005) *The State of the World's Children,* New York: UNICEF.

World Development Report (2004) *Making Services Work for Poor People,* Washington DC: World Bank.

Education and skills

Hertz, B and G Sperling (2004) *What Works in Girls' Education: Evidence and Policy from the Developing World,* New York: Council on Foreign Relations.

UNESCO *Education for All Global Monitoring Report 2004: The Quality Imperative*, Paris: UNESCO.

Delivering healthcare

AU/NEPAD (2003) *Health Strategy*, Midrand: New Partnership for Africa's Development Secretariat (NEPAD).

The Copenhagen Consensus (2004) www.copenhagen consensus.com

Joint Learning Initiative (2004) *The JLI Strategy Report: Human Resources for Health: Overcoming the Crisis*, Boston: Harvard University Press www.globalhealthtrust.org/Report.html

Water and Sanitation

WSSCC (2004) *Water, Sanitation and Hygiene (WASH) Campaign Factsheet*, Geneva: Water Supply and Sanitation Collaborative Council.

HIV and AIDS

Barnett, T and A Whiteside (2002) *AIDS in the Twenty-First Century: Disease and Globalisation*, Palgrave Macmillan.

UNAIDS (2004) *Report on the Global HIV and AIDS epidemic: 4th Global Report*, Geneva: UNAIDS.

Tackling exclusion and vulnerability

Barrientos, A and J De Jong (2004) *Child Poverty and Cash Transfers*, CHIP report no 4.

Devereux, S and R Sabetes-Wheeler (2004) *Transformative Social Protection*. IDS working paper 232, Brighton: Institute of Development Studies.

Chapter 7. Going for growth

General reading

Bloom, D and J Sachs (1998) 'Geography, Demography and Economic Growth in Africa', in *Brookings Papers on Economic Activity*, 207–295.

Chen, S and M Ravallion (2004) *How Have the World's Poorest Fared since the Early 1980s?*, World Bank Policy Research Working Paper 3341, June 2004.

Fafchamps, M, F Teal and J Toyne (2001) *Towards a growth strategy for Africa*, Oxford: Centre for Study of African Economies.

Rodrik, D (2003) *Growth Strategies*, Centre for Economic Policy Research, Discussion Paper Series, 4100, October 2003.

Stern, N, J J Dethier and F Halsey Rogers (2005) *Growth and Empowerment: Making Development Happen,* MIT Press, Cambridge.

World Bank (2000) *Can Africa Claim the 21st Century*, Washington DC: World Bank.

A safe place to invest

World Bank (2004a) *World Development Report 2005: A Better Investment Climate For All*, Washington DC: World Bank.

World Bank (2004b) *Doing Business in 2004: Understanding Regulations*, Oxford: OUP.

Improving infrastructure

African Development Bank (1999) *African Development Bank Report 1999: Infrastructure Development in Africa*, New York: Oxford.

InterAcademy Council. Intergovernmental panel on climate change (IPCC, 2001a) *Climate Change 2001: Impacts, Adaptation and Vulnerability. Summary for policy makers*, Third Assessment Report, UNEP/WMO.

Down on the farm

AU/NEPAD (2003) *Comprehensive Africa Agriculture Development Programme*, Midrand: New Partnership for Africa's Development (NEPAD).

The challenge of urbanisation

Tibaijuka, A (2005) *Africa on the move: an urban crisis in the making*, paper prepared for the Commission for Africa: UN-HABITAT. Available at www.commissionforafrica.org

The environment and climate change

UNEP (2003) *Development of an Action Plan for the Environment Initiative of NEPAD. Combating Climate Change in Africa*, Nairobi: UNEP.

Involving poor people in growth

OECD (2004) *Accelerating Pro-Poor Growth through Support for Private Sector Development*, Emerging Market Economics Paper for OECD DAC PovNet.

UN Commission on the Private Sector and Development (2004) *Unleashing Entrepreneurship: Making Business Work for The Poor*, New York: UNDP.

Chapter 8. More trade and fairer trade

General reading

UNDP (2003) *Making Global Trade Work For People*, New York.

World Bank (2002) Global Economic Prospects and the Developing Countries 2002: *Making Trade Work for the World's Poor*, Washington DC: World Bank.

World Bank (2003) Global Economic Prospects 2004: *Realizing the Development Promise of the Doha Agenda Development*, Washington DC: World Bank.

Increasing Africa's capacity to trade

UNCTAD (2003a) *Economic Development In Africa: Trade Performance and Commodity Dependence,* New York: United Nations.

Opportunities for trade

Hinkle, L and M Schiff (2004) *Economic Partnership Agreements between sub-Saharan Africa and the EU: A Development Perspective on their Trade Components.* Draft Africa Region Working Paper, Washington DC: World Bank.

Messerlin, P A (2004) *Forging a Deal on Agricultural Trade Reform: Scenario Paper.* Briefing note for the June 8–9th Conference on Breaking the Deadlock in Agricultural Trade Reform and Development, Centre for Global Studies, Oxford University.

Stevens, C and J Kennan (2004) *Comparative Study of G8 Preferential Access Schemes for Africa.* Institute of Development Studies.

Chapter 9. Where will the money come from?

General reading

Devarajan, S, D Dollar and T Holmgren (2002) *Aid & Reform in Africa – Lessons from 10 case studies,* Washington DC: World Bank.

Foster, M (2003) *The Case for Increased Aid,* DFID final report: London.

Does Aid work?

Collier, P and D Dollar (2004) 'Development Effectiveness: What have we learnt?', *Economic Journal*, 114: 244–271.

ECA and OECD/DAC (2005) *2005 Mutual Review Report*, Economic Commission for Africa and Organisation for Economic Co-operation and Development/Development Assistance Committee: Addis Ababa and Paris.

McGillivray, M (2004) *Is Aid Effective?*, WIDER: Helsinki.

How much Aid can Africa usefully absorb?

Clemens, M, S Radelet and R Bhavnani (2004) *Counting Chickens when they hatch: the short term effect of aid on growth*, Center for Global Development Working Paper No. 44, Center for Global Development: Washington DC.

World Bank (2004) *Aid Effectiveness and Financing Modalities*, Annual Meetings Paper for discussion by the Development Committee, October 2, Washington DC: World Bank.

Is extra Aid forever?

Lancaster, C and S Wangwe (2000) *Managing a Smooth Transition from Aid Dependence in Africa*, Economic Development Policy Essay, Overseas Development Council, Johns Hopkins University Press: Baltimore.

What about debt?

Martin, M et al. (2004) *Long-Term Debt Sustainability for Africa*, background paper prepared for the Commission for Africa, Debt Relief International: London.

Raising the money

HM Treasury and DFID (2004) *IFF Brochure*, London.

Landau, J P et al. (2004) *Groupe de Travail sur les nouvelles contributions financières internationales – rapport à Monsieur Jacques Chirac Président de la République*, English version, septembre 2004: Paris.

Chapter 10. Making it happen

African Development Forum (2004) *ADF IV Final Report*, final report of the African Development Forum IV, 11–15 October 2004, Addis Ababa, Ethiopia, accessed via www.uneca.org/adf

Collier, P (1997) The failure of conditionality, in Gwin, C and J Nelson (eds), *Perspectives on Aid and Development*, Washington DC: Overseas Development Council.

Elbadawi, I and J Randa (2003) *Beyond Good Policy: Quality of Aid and Growth*, mimeo, World Bank Development Economic Research Group: Washington DC.

Kanbur, R (2000) Aid, Conditionality and Debt in Africa, Chapter 18 in Tarp, F (ed) *Foreign Aid and Development*, Routledge, London and New York.

Odero, K, P Njenga and M Mashiri (2004) *Mechanisms, Processes and Stages of Reviewing the Performance of External Development Partners*, NEPAD Discussion Paper, CSIR: Transportek Consortium, December 2004, Pretoria, South Africa.

OECD/DAC (2005) *Paris Declaration on Aid Effectiveness*, OECD/DAC High Level Forum, Paris, February 28– March 2, 2005, accessed via www.aidharmonisation.org

PENGUIN POLITICS

THE END OF POVERTY
JEFFREY SACHS

FOREWORD BY BONO

'The ideas in this book have a hook you won't forget: the end of poverty ... In Jeff's hands, the millstone of opportunity around our necks becomes an adventure, something doable and achievable' Bono

WE CAN END POVERTY BY 2025 ... AND CHANGE THE WORLD FOREVER.

For the first time in history, our generation has the opportunity to end extreme poverty in the world's most desperate nations. But how can we stop the cycle of bad health, bad debt, and bad luck that holds back more than a billion people?

Jeffrey D. Sachs, Special Advisor to UN Secretary-General Kofi Annan and 'probably the most important economist in the world' (*The New York Times*) has the answers. He has visited and worked in over 100 countries across the globe – from Africa to India, Poland to Bolivia – advising leaders on economic development and poverty reduction. Here he lays out how poverty has been beaten in the past, how – in realistic, attainable steps – we can make a real difference for the one-fifth of humanity who still live in extreme poverty, how they can find partnership with their wealthy counterparts, how little it will actually cost, and how everyone can help.

The End of Poverty is a roadmap to a more prosperous and secure world.